Our Journey

50 Years Seeking to Follow Jesus

Peter Butt

DEDICATION

To my incredible wife who has been alongside me for over 50 years of this journey, supporting me as we have served the Lord together.

It is also dedicated to my 4 children who have been part of this journey. Thank you, Susanne, Juliet, Frances, and Andrew.

It is also dedicated to everyone who appears in its pages. You have been part of the journey!

PETER BUTT

CONTENTS

COMMENDATIONS

John Noble Author, Christian ministry, and Chairman of the UK National Charismatic & Pentecostal Leaders Conference 1984 - 2006

I have known Peter and Irene for many years when we have been friends and co-workers together, and I am fully aware that their great passion is to inspire, embolden and release men and women into everything the Lord has prepared for them. So, I know that Peter has not written this remarkable story of their journey and God's provision so that you might stand back in admiration and say, "wow, what a great couple!" Rather that you see they are just two ordinary people who have learned to trust an extraordinary God! This gives us all hope and the belief that what our amazing God did for them, he can also do for you and me!

Paul Randerson – Brecklands Christian Fellowships, East Anglia.

"Our lives as Christians are important in that we not only live in the wonderful providence of God but that we are also able to impact others around us on the way. In knowing Peter and Irene for many years this book is a real, practical, faith filled record of their journey. It encourages us all to pray, to hear and act on Gods prophetic words. Their obedience has blessed and continues to bless new generations to rise up and be all they can be. Many people in this book, who touched Peter and Irene's lives are no longer with us. They were giants in the land. May a new generation be stirred to arise on journeys of faith and obedience."

Rev Ian Jennings - Associate Minister St Marys Denham.

I have known Peter Butt since we were students together at Bible College. That was more than fifty years ago, and we have remained friends ever since. I stand in awe at all that God has accomplished through Peter and Irene. The vision that first inspired them so long ago has been brought to fulfilment over a lifetime of faithful ministry and single-minded obedience to God's call. The story of that journey is beautifully told in this book. It is an Inspiring book. I am sure it will inspire faith in all who are serious about hearing from God and walking in his will.

Roger Blackmore – Senior Pastor Genesis Church, Long Island, New York. USA.

I am glad that my dear friend Peter Butt decided to write this book. With a lifetime of ministry comes a wealth of experience and it is only right to make some of that available to others. He has trained thousands of leaders worldwide and this volume is a continuation of his commitment to equipping and inspiring others. A few years ago, I commented to Peter that there were some outstanding young leaders in today's Christian church. He readily agreed and then wryly commented, "But we've got something they haven't – we've got decades of stories!" We certainly have. And we're enriched by Peter sharing some of his in 'Our Journey'.

INTRODUCTION

Having reached the grand old age of 73 and thinking my writing days are over, I was recently challenged, as I shared a few stories of the way God has prophetically led Irene and me, to record these stories in a book to encourage another generation.

This came following several conversations with others over the past couple of years. Whilst sharing with some friends of ours during a meal in their home, our friend Lyn said, "you must record these stories for people to hear".

Believing the scriptures that suggest "two, better three witnesses confirm and establish the truth", it was at a wedding that we were challenged in the same way. Sitting at a table with friends who had been touched by God at our youth camp ministry in the late 70's and 80's, we shared memories of how God had moved in those days. It was suggested by one of the guys that we should write the stories down.

There was one man at the table whom I did not know and had never met, he had been introduced to me as being prophetic. Following this conversation, in a rather casual way, I asked him if he had a word from the Lord for me. He immediately replied Yes! and felt that it was important to recount the stories of what God had done in so many lives in those years.

So here we are. I am looking to achieve 3 things:

1. Tell the story of our journey emphasising the faithfulness, goodness, mercy, grace, and love of God. Why **our** journey? My wife and I and our children experienced this journey but more than that it seeks to reveal that God was and is with us. He is the cause of our journey and the senior partner in our journey.

2. To inspire another generation to continue to expect God to work in a way relevant to their culture and context. It may be an encouragement to read the stories and make a few notes. Maybe you will feel challenged in some area, why not write down your response. I have included some "Things to ponder" at the end of each chapter.

3. To place on record the story of "The Sussex Pentecostal Youth Camps" and "School of Ministries International".

I recently came across this quote:

> *"The art of storytelling is the most powerful weapon in the war of ideas"* - Carmine Gallo.

My friend from South Africa, Roger Pearce, makes this comment in his book "Better Together":

> *"Stories have tremendous power, Stories are powerful as they connect us to others, they create emotional connections that connect our hearts to*

one another. As we unpack the feelings and emotions associated with a story, we get to understand why things are as they are. Stories shape our identity for good or bad depending on which stories we are listening to"

At the event celebrating our stepping down from leadership of the ministry we had founded and been leading for 25 years, our friend, Paul Randerson prophesied, "There is another book inside you on faith, it is for others around the world. It is more inspiration than instruction."

This is the story of that journey.

1

THE BEGINNING

*Ps 139:13-16 "You are the one who put me together
inside my mother's body, and I praise you because
of the wonderful way you created me. Everything
you do is marvelous, of this I have no
doubt. Nothing about me is hidden from you! I was
secretly woven together deep in the earth below, but
with your own eyes you saw my body being formed.
Even before I was born, you had written in your
book everything I would do."*

Providence

Many of you who know me will not be surprised that I start
with a theological matter. There is a doctrine called, "The
Providence of God"; it states that God is involved in
working, leading directing, arranging events in our lives that

are related to His purpose for us. It is expressed throughout the scriptures in the Old Testament in such verses as:
Psalm 37:23, "The steps of a good man are ordered by the Lord; and He delights in his way",

and in the New Testament:

Roms 8:28. "And we know that all things work together for good to those who love God, to those who are called according to His purpose".

God works in our lives arranging Divine appointments and connections that influence and affect our lives. It is always of interest to me when people testify to their coming to faith how God has "arranged" for them to work next to a Christian who shared their faith or led them to a house next door to a believer.

Of course, there are many stories out there that we never get to hear because people choose to reject the message! As I look back over my life, I see evidence of the providence of God.

Godly Midwives.

I was born in 1948 in Oldchurch Hospital, Romford. In the late 1970's I went to a meeting where I heard two missionary ladies share their story. They had been midwives in Ghana serving the Lord. They had been instrumental in seeing significant numbers of African people come to the Lord. They advertised a book they had written of their adventures called "They Two went on….." Their names were Eva Davidson and Ann Symonds. I was so impressed with them that I acquired a copy of the book and read their story. Can you image my surprise and response when I read that they had trained as midwives from 1946-1949 in Oldchurch Hospital, Romford! They then went on to say that they held every baby that was born in their arms and prayed for them that God would take hold of their lives and use them. I was overwhelmed as I realised that I was one of those babies!

At times when I consider this, I am moved to tears. I shared this in a church meeting in Nottingham, where a guy called David Shearman was the leader, he cried out behind me with the words, "So was I". That's providence.

My Name

My parents were Christians and named me Peter Andrew after the disciples of Jesus. I guess they had aspirations for me. My older brother was named Stephen Victor after the martyr in the book of Acts known as Stephen the Victor! It did not really impact me much until a few years ago. I was involved in a telephone call to discuss a bill I had received. I was rather frustrated and a little annoyed as it had taken me quite a few minutes to get through to the correct department.

Eventually I reached the person who could deal with my problem, and the lady requested my name. I said Peter Andrew Butt and her reply took me by surprise. She said, "O very biblical". I asked if she was a Christian and she replied that she had recently come into a relationship with Jesus because of an Alpha course. We resolved the outstanding issue, and I completed the call and put down the telephone. As I did so, I suddenly became aware of the prophetic significance of my name.

I realised I had become what my parents had believed for me all those years ago. Through the providence of God, I had been led into church leadership which I guess was in the heart of my mother and father and their prayer all those years ago.

Ron and Mary Byatt

For a period in the 1950's, our family attended an evangelical church in Harold Hill, Essex. Although I had made a commitment to follow Jesus as a child, in those days I was more a follower of Tottenham Hotspur who were the football team of the late 50's and early 60's. Living within reach of the ground and having friends at school who were also into football, my life consisted of playing football and following Spurs. However, there were a couple in the church who made a great impact upon me.

Mary was a nurse, preparing to marry and then go with her husband, Ron, to Nepal as missionaries with the RBMU (Regions Beyond Missionary Union). Ron was away at university training to be a doctor and not often at the church. Mary had a great voice and would often sing and testify how things were going. I was intrigued by this couple and admired them greatly.

In those days there were only a couple of churches in Nepal, and it was before the days of easy travel. I thought they were very brave and courageous and even in my young mind I was aware of the sacrifice they were making. They become heroes of mine.

It was about 10 years ago that I was first privileged to travel to Nepal to the NIM church in Gyaneshwar, Kathmandu. I preached to a full church of some 1500 people; this was the third service of the day. NIM had planted many churches around the region and into the nation. As I stood looking over this congregation I was moved to tears as I remembered Ron and Mary. Something stirred in my spirit from those childhood days, and I thanked God for the privilege of seeing what He had done in this nation.

I had this sense that it was no accident, that I was present to see what God was doing. It impacted me greatly and when I mentioned Ron and Mary, I discovered that Ron had compiled the first hymn book in the Nepali language.

Again, I saw evidence of God being involved in my life in a providential way. Touching my heart as a young boy for the nations.

Willie Burton

I was around 11 years of age when my father encouraged me to go to a Monday evening meeting at a church in Brentwood, Essex to hear a missionary called Willie Burton. I had no interest in spending my mid-week evening at a church meeting. However, I went along with some reservation.

We arrived a few minutes late and the only seats available were on the front row. There was nothing unusual about the gathering until Willie Burton began to speak. He had been instrumental in seeing a remarkable move of the Holy Spirit in Zaire (previously known as Belgian Congo).

Some 1000 churches had been planted, marked by an extraordinary release of miracles and healing. He told some intriguing and exciting accounts of God working in that nation and then decided to illustrate how they had saved a young boy from drowning in a river by forming a human chain. He looked around the congregation for people of appropriate size and stature to reproduce this drama, and the first person he chose was me.

I was embarrassed and a little unsure but went to the front to be part of this exercise. I put my arms around his ample body and along with others enacted this scene. At the end of the scene, he turned to me, put his hand on my head and said something that I did not pick up or remember.

Around 15 years ago, on one of our regular visits to South Africa, a guy called John, who had been born and bred in Congo, requested that I visit his nation. I ignored his request as we were already overstretched. However, each year following he persisted, saying that there were many churches ready and waiting for us to visit with teaching and training.

Eventually, he wore me down and I began to ask for more information. I discovered that these churches had been part of the network formed by Willie Burton and that in recent years there had been a dearth of teaching and training. I visited on two occasions and again had that overwhelming sense of God being active in "arranging" circumstances for me to visit these amazing churches.

I guess one day I might meet Willie Burton in heaven and ask him what he said. I am convinced my visit to that nation was in the purpose of God for me.

Baptism

I was a late comer when it came to water baptism. I had made a decision to follow Jesus as a young boy but got lost in my pursuit of football and friends and being a teenager in the 60's.

At the age of 16 I fully surrendered to Jesus and all He had for me. I thank God that I never got too involved in stuff that could have damaged my life; it was the grace and providence of God and the prayers of my parents.

However, I had not been baptised in water. I had been filled with the Holy Spirit and was following Jesus and involved in all the meetings and activities of the church. I had met Irene, who eventually became my wife, and was getting on with my life and relationship with God. However, water baptism had become an embarrassment to me as I was now 18 years of age and wanting to move on in the things of God. I bit the bullet and was baptised in water imagining that everyone was muttering under their breath, "I didn't realise he was not baptised, that is a surprise".

In those days, I had perhaps shared one or two things from the scripture in some open meetings, but I had never preached and had no inkling that God would call me to be a teacher of the Word of God. It was the custom on those occasions, to give those who had been baptised a certificate and at the bottom there was a place for a bible verse. My father chose that verse for me. It was:

Joshua 1:8 "This Book of the Law shall not depart from your mouth, but you shall meditate on it day and night, so that you may be careful to do according to all that is written in it. For then you will make your way prosperous, and then you will have good success."

I do not know if he had it in his heart for me to be a preacher and teacher of scripture, but it is remarkable that this has been the major focus of over 50 years of public ministry. It is the only verse in the Bible that include the words prosperous and success in the same sentence. God knew what was in His heart for me and arranged these moments of challenge in His purpose and plan for my life.

I am convinced that there are many who can testify to extraordinary Divine interventions in their lives and the providential dealings of God that have resulted in them finding and following Jesus. I am not more special than anybody else and suggest it is a good exercise to meditate on the "providence of God" and to recognise and thank Him for His working in our lives.

Thoughts to ponder: *Where is the evidence of the Providence of God in your life?*

2

CALL TO MINISTRY

Jer 1:5 "Before I formed you in the womb I knew you, and before you were born, I consecrated you; I appointed you a prophet to the nations."

Salvation

Sunday evening in my childhood we often spent at home with my mother, as my father attended the gospel service at Brentwood Road Evangelical Church, Romford. We always wanted to go with my father, not for the meeting but because he always visited someone afterwards and we would get to be out later than usual.

However, one evening was different. I was not particularly taking notice of the preacher until he started to personally challenge the congregation whether they had a relationship with God, whether their sin had been dealt with, whether they had invited Jesus to be part of their lives.

I was only 6 or 7 years of age; I had not robbed any banks or committed any terrible crimes, but I knew I did not have a relationship with God, and I felt an extraordinary sense of guilt and knew I needed to resolve this matter. I squirmed as the appeal was given and tried to hide behind the pew because I thought the preacher was looking directly at me. I did not manage to respond and felt ashamed and concerned because of that.

Most evenings my father would come to the bedroom I shared with my brother and pray with us. I plucked up the courage to say to him, "Dad I should have prayed that prayer tonight to invite Jesus into my life." My father replied, "That's alright son you can do it now" and he then prayed with me, and I knew the work was done. Even now, 65 years later, I can remember that moment and know that I became a believer in Jesus and that I was forgiven.

As I look back to my teenage years, I recognise how God began to work on my heart and mind to prepare me for ministry. At the same time, he was at work in Irene's life, to bring us to a place of seeking His will for our lives above our own aspirations and desires.

Following school, I worked in a national bank. We had plans to get married, buy a house and all the other normal things a couple would aspire to. However, we found ourselves increasingly involved in the local church, taking on responsibilities in music ministry and working among the children. At one time we had approached the leadership of the church to commence a mid-week children's club and were attending conferences and meetings where we were challenged to serve the Lord.

Bryn Eirias

It was at a Christian holiday centre in North Wales where our journey began to take shape. I had enjoyed a holiday at this place in my mid-teens and been challenged about my need of being filled with the Holy Spirit.

Although it is 50 years ago, I can remember the challenge. "Do you struggle to live how you know God wants you to live; do you feel unworthy and helpless even though you want to follow Jesus; if so, you need to be filled with the Holy Spirit".

It was like a prophetic arrow that went straight to my heart. There was an immediate "Yes!" and I responded to the invitation to be filled with the Spirit. I was prayed for and quietly but clearly, as I was encouraged, I began to speak with other languages as I received the Holy Spirit. I left that meeting place feeling elated and excited by my relationship with God.

Before being filled with the Spirit, Jesus had seemed so far away even though I knew I was a believer and had experienced salvation. Now it was as if He were by my side and that I could touch him, so real was His presence at that moment. The baptism of the Holy Spirit transformed my life and relationship with God.

For the next few years, we made an annual pilgrimage to this holiday centre and always experienced an encounter with God that finally led to a significant one that changed the course of our lives. We had taken two weeks annual leave but only booked for one week at Bryn Eirias. At the end of the week, we returned home to Essex.

There was a holy dissatisfaction in my spirit, and I felt we should have stayed another week as God wanted to speak with us. Irene and I had some frank conversations as she was initially reluctant to return, but we agreed to go back and, on the Monday, made our way to Colwyn Bay.

The first evening meeting, the preacher spoke on the bible verse *"Take up your cross and follow me" Mark 8:34*

Irene and I were in tears. A young couple called Steve and Molly whom we had met several years before were also present that week; they had just become involved in church leadership having responded to the call of God.

We spent some time talking with them and felt a stirring in our spirits. The second night another preacher spoke on the same verse and a third evening resulted in a call to surrender our lives to the will and purpose of God.

We returned home completely convinced that God was calling us to serve Him in some form of ministry. Irene then returned to work at the centre in Wales for several months.

Bible College

We began to seek God and he began to speak to us. Irene felt she should pursue working amongst children and went through the necessary training for that work. She completed her studies and began working in a Children's home in Brentwood, Essex.

As I pursued the Lord it was as if everywhere I turned God presented me with the challenge to go to Bible College. I would look at an article in a magazine or book and knew even before I read that I would read something that would be a sign that God was guiding me in this way. I would have conversations and find them ending with a suggestion that maybe God was leading me to take this next step.

I began the process of applying to a Bible College and was accepted. Even though I was approaching 20 years of age, I felt it was important to acquire my father's approval. When I spoke with him to ask his permission, he was insistent that it was not necessary to attend Bible School. He said that if God had called me, I should spend time seeking Him at home and using my evenings to study and pray. He refused to bless my decision. I prayed and felt God wanted me to honour my parents, so I let my place for the next term at the college lapse.

Several weeks later my father and I were in the same meeting in another church that was not our local meeting place. A leader we knew who was involved in yet another church was also present, and he brought a prophetic word in that meeting. It was probably a word of knowledge that today would have been given to an individual, but in those days the gifts of the Spirit were only shared in the public arena.

He said that God had called someone to go away to study, that they were to go over the water. (We were in Essex the college was in Surrey which meant we had to go over the Thames). He said that God would open the way and provide the means for the will of God to be fulfilled. That night when I returned home my father simply said, "You can go".

He had heard God speak and responded to allow me to maintain my integrity and not disobey my parents in the pursuit of God's purpose for my life. I have used that illustration on various occasions to indicate that if God is leading you, He will remove every obstacle and allow you to retain your integrity to bring about His purpose.

Those two years at Bible College, with all its limitations, were extremely important in my development and preparation for what God had for me. After a few weeks all my own thoughts about my "ministry" were demolished.

Back home I had been the "bright, young thing" now I was just one among many and I became aware of my spiritual poverty as I rubbed shoulders with many young men and women who were miles ahead of me in terms of their relationship with God, their understanding of the scriptures and their capacity for sharing the truth of God in outreach and church meetings.

I felt backslidden, and after seven weeks faced a serious challenge, either I had to get serious or give up. God had called me. I now needed to prove my calling. I made the decision to miss lunch every day and read the Bible. This gave me an hour to "catch up" and get to know the scriptures and the God of the book. I read the Bible through every term while I was at the College, which started a pattern for my life that continues to this day.

I read the Bible through 5 times in those two years, and since then have read the Bible through every year at least once. It was at Bible College that I began to learn lessons of faith and to trust God for finance.

I made some great friends at that time and still after over 50 years am in contact with them and involved in ministry with others.

Thought to ponder: *What has God called you to be and then to do? What steps do you need to take to see the fulfilment of Gods purpose in your life?*

3

CHURCH LEADERSHIP

Eph 4:11,12. "And truly He gave some to be apostles, and some to be prophets, and some to be evangelists, and some to be pastors and teachers, for the perfecting of the saints, for the work of the ministry, for the edifying of the body of Christ.

Pastor, Alston Chapel, Barnet

Our first ministry appointment was in Barnet, North London. A small church which had been through some serious difficulties was our first challenge. We survived five years and in the final year saw a breakthrough in growth and fruitfulness. We married in August 1970 and commenced leading the church in September 1970. We had three children in 4 years and lived in a very poor quality, basement flat, but God provided for us in wonderful and exciting ways.

When we first arrived, the church could only offer us a very small salary which paid half the rent of the place in which we were living. I knew that if I was to build the church, I

19

would need time to pray, prepare and pastor the people. I felt that I should not take on full time employment but look for work for two days a week. I had clerical and accounting skills from my days in the bank so visited the local employment agency to seek work.

The lady who interviewed me was very sure that I would not be able to find the kind of work I was seeking. She was experienced over many years in this work and said in all her years such a part-time opportunity had never arisen. I left the office a little despondent but still determined to press on.

I had several other people to visit and so returned home about three hours later. In those days we did not have a telephone in our home. As I opened the door Irene, my wife, excitedly told me that some time before a lady had called at our home from the employment agency I had visited. She told my wife that as soon as I left the office, she received a call from a company asking if they had someone competent in administrative work and simple accounting for a two day a week appointment. She was so overwhelmed and excited that she visited our home during her lunch hour to convey the news to us. This was a brilliant answer to our prayer and another sign of God going before us.

We spent five years building the church, completed a new building programme and left the church with its first full-time leader and three times the size it had been when we first took on the leadership.

During our time in Barnet, I preached three times a week: a Sunday morning exhortation and encouragement; a Sunday evening gospel message; and a Thursday evening Bible

Study. It was tough but I believe the foundations laid in those years provided me with the resources from which the teaching ministry I exercise has developed over these past 50 years.

Three years into our time in Barnet, God spoke to me prophetically.[1] This led us to work alongside Norman Young, the senior pastor of the church in Walthamstow.

Pastor, Walthamstow

Again, with hindsight I see the wisdom and providence of God in giving us three years in East London at Emmanuel Hall, Walthamstow. We enjoyed working with a senior leader. Norman Young was a very experienced man of God and taught us so much in those years. We also built relationship with a group of people who became involved with us in our young camp work.

It was during this time that the camp ministry we were involved with from the beginning began to expand beyond our expectations and led to a challenge to us about our priorities and vision. We realised that we could not lead the church and run this growing youth camp work and so felt God speak into our situation yet again. This led us into a commitment to work with youth from across the nation.[2]

Leadership Team, Corringham

Again, through a series of events recorded in the chapters on houses and prophetic direction we found ourselves in

---

[1] See Chapter 5. Prophetic Direction – Walthamstow.
[2] See Chapter 5. Prophetic Direction – Camp. Chapter 6. Camp – from small beginnings.

Corringham, Essex. Expecting to stay for one or two years, we stayed for nine years between 1978 and 1987. The church in the UK was being challenged at that time by a move of the Holy Spirit which resulted in new churches being formed variously known as "house churches", "the Restoration movement" and "New churches". We were influenced by this movement, and I was delighted to be invited by Mike Godward, the senior leader of the work to be part of the leadership team.

We enjoyed a season of new life and new growth as God opened up to us new understanding on a number of issues. Church life and practice which is second nature today was cutting edge and new in those days; small groups; apostolic ministry; open worship with guitars and drums; extended public worship sessions; relationships at a new level and creativity released in the church in fresh and dynamic ways are just some of the things we discovered and experienced.

The church grew significantly and although I was involved with the youth camp work, being part of the team with responsibility for teaching the Word of God enabled me to function effectively. These were exciting years and Irene and our children enjoyed that season.

My first international trip took place during our time in Corringham. In 1986 when I was invited to visit Jamaica. We went to teach in the churches and in the Assemblies of God Bible College. Along with Paul Randerson I spent 3 weeks on the island preaching, teaching, and training. It was a remarkable time and led to invitations to return.

Over the years I have visited Jamaica more than 20 times. In more recent days I would visit in February and teach at the

Western Jamaica Teaching Conference and the CFAN Bible School.

It was during this time, that the senior leadership team was invited by the apostolic team led by Bryn Jones to visit his ministry centre in Keighley, Yorkshire, and spend some time with a group of prophetic people to hear what God might be saying to us as a team and a church. This resulted in a life-changing, direction-changing experience for me.[3]

Brentwood and Team Spirit.

We next found ourselves relocating to Brentwood to be closer to the apostolic team led by John Noble, called Team Spirit. I took on an administrative role with the team and became involved with the work. John, at that time was a highly respected national church leader and the chairman of the National Charismatic Leaders Conference.

I was introduced into this national movement and met many significant and powerful leaders during those years. The Brentwood church we connected with became part of a joining of several churches under the leadership of David Matthews, and I became part of that team.

In response to the prophetic word concerning teaching and training I commenced leadership training courses at Pilgrims Hall as part of Team Spirit. We saw many leaders emerge into their ministry during those times. I also recall several prophetic words during this season concerning training leaders. We also saw the miraculous provision of a church building.

---

[3] See Chapter 5. Prophetic Direction – Leadership Training.

During these years we were very involved in a successful Christian conference and holiday event over the Spring Bank Holiday weekend. We saw thousands of people touched, blessed, and transformed during some powerful times of encounter with the Holy Spirit. Great preaching and a great venue, the Brentwood International Centre provided the framework for this event over many years. This was a fruitful time of ministry and building of relationships which stand to this day.

As a result of the link with John Noble and the National Charismatic conference we were invited to be involved with an international leader's conference in Brighton in 1991. We made many new connections and received many invitations to visit other nations. One of those was with South Africa. I was part of a team that visited South Africa in 1992 and then in December of that year we began our first training sessions in Lujizweni, South Africa. It was a remarkable trip.

This network of some 160 churches had come into being because of a move of the Holy Spirit. When we arrived, we were told we were the fulfilment of a prophetic word they had received some years before. That leaders from overseas would come and teach and train them. They had even built "rondavels" (mud huts) to house these teachers. They believed we were the fulfilment of that word. Again, as School of Ministries developed, we connected with several networks of leaders and have since visited on numerous occasions to teach and train leaders.

It was also during this season that I was invited to visit Kenya and Uganda in 1993. We began teaching and training sessions with groups in Kisumu and Kampala. This developed over the years to become one of the most fruitful and expansive of the School of Ministries programmes with many centres and even other countries embracing the training programme.

Events outside of our control led to John Noble moving to Cobham in Surrey and Team Spirit being subsumed within the Pioneer Network under the leadership of Gerald Coates. This left us in a place of uncertainty but there was a clarity that this was not the way for us, and that the call to teach and train leaders was the priority for our lives.

Southampton

During this season we met Tony Morton from Southampton, leader of the Cornerstone network. We became involved with him and the churches over a period of 18 months to 2 years. Tony was very warm and friendly towards us and invited us to become involved with the Cornerstone Team. This led us to move to the South Coast and for over 25 years we have been living in Southampton. This was a very significant move for us. [4]

Thought to ponder: *Am I willing to move house or locality to be part of the church body that God has called me to be part of?*

---

[4] See Chapter 5. Prophetic Direction – Southampton.

4

TEACHING AND TRAINING

2 Tim 4:2. "Preach the Word, be instant in season and out of season, reprove, rebuke, exhort with all long-suffering and doctrine."

School of Ministries

We arrived in Southampton with the intention of seeing the work of teaching and training develop. We had visited Australia in 1995 and seen the effectiveness of teaching and training programmes in the local church in the CLC churches in Sydney, in both the Waterloo church led by Frank Houston and Hills church led by Brian Houston.

I had recognised the weakness of the Bible College model and been looking for a way to develop a more discipleship-based, local church based, model of training. My friend, Robert Ferguson had invited us to teach in the Aquila School of Ministries and opened doors for us to visit the Hills training school. We came back inspired by what we saw and with a vision to see a more local or regional leadership training model.

We commenced School of Ministries in Southampton and with the help of Phil Orchard and Jean Brand and the support of Tony Morton, the apostolic leader of the Cornerstone Network we were able to carry out a year-long training programme comprising of 36 ten-hour modules.

The teacher's notes, student notes and audio recordings were all prepared in that first year. The different gifts and ministries in the network made contributions to the course which in effect was a Bible College curriculum but with a much more practical application.

This developed into another course called "Deeper in the Word" where we took 12 modules as a basic training unit. We saw many sign up from the local church, the region and even a few from further afield to take part in "Deeper" as it became known.

Over 5 or 6 years we saw this programme help many people and encourage many others. Some are now leaders in churches around the world. Up to this point it was only operating in the UK. In my mind I still imagined a static school perhaps with people visiting and taking part from overseas.

SOM Development

As a result of the international work of Cornerstone I visited India in 1995, prior to our move to Southampton. One of our first "official" School of Ministries schools was in Mumbai. We had over 500 leaders in attendance, this became the first of an on-going and growing work in this vast nation.

Our apostolic friend, Basil became the host for this work, and we found ourselves visiting centres across the country. Basil reports that we have trained over 12000 leaders in India. We also began to see the growth of our work in Uganda and Kenya at this time.

We had been on several overseas trips teaching and training but the nature of our responsibilities in the UK restricted when we were able to travel. Billy Kennedy became the leader of the church and the network and suggested to me the time had come to lay down the Deeper programme as he felt they needed a broader teaching and training programme.

My initial response was quite negative, and it felt like the ministry was shutting down. I spent a night tossing and turning and thinking over the whole matter. In the morning I awoke and began to consider the prophetic words that had been given to me about teaching, training, and travel. I realised this new season would give me the opportunity to see the fulfilment of the directional words we had been given concerning travelling to the nations. It was as if a light was switched on and the Lord had presented me with an open door of opportunity.

I was around 60 years of age and it struck me very forcefully that if I did not do it now, I would look back with regret at having missed a "Kairos" moment. This was the beginning of the development of SOM International and resulted in many nations opening up to us, with schools expanding across the world. We also at that time received extraordinary prophetic encouragement.[5]

Prophetic Direction

As you will see in the next chapter, School of Ministries is the outworking of the prophetic words given to us over several decades. We began in a small way and have seen the work progress in a remarkable way. Our decisions have always been based on what we feel God has said to us.

Pursuing the Vision

In the pursuit of the vision to see leaders across the globe taught and trained, God has brought together a brilliant team of gifted, anointed and committed leaders. Graham Bower felt the Lord was leading him to make a commitment to the work and became a major support in the work.

Kay Gill took up the prayer challenge; Basil D'Souza became the director of the work in Asia and Graham took up Africa. Eric Skates initially took on the development of materials and training, later stepping back, and Phil Orchard took up that role. Katrina Mack offered her services in an administrative role and later took on prayer from Kay.

Rob Lee from Cardiff, who had been with us on trips in the early 90's before SOM came into being, has taken up the promotions and fund-raising role. Graham Blake has now taken on the African role and Lucie Rush covers the administration for Africa.

---

[5] See Chapter 5. Prophetic Direction – School of Ministries.

This team, supported by an advisory group, have provided the foundation for the ministry to grow.

Listening to the Spirit

One of the most important aspects of this work has been listening to what the Holy Spirit is saying to us. We have sought to keep an open ear to the next step to take and found that God has led us, sometimes in direct prophetic ways and often through that still small voice where we find a common agreement to move ahead in the team. The prayer foundation has meant that God has opened doors for SOM without major advertising or promotion. We have also spent more time praying about the provision of finance than appealing for funds.

Meeting up with people and re-commencing relationships has opened major doors of opportunity for us. In my early days of ministry, I built a great relationship with Clive Beckenham and Jim Palmer. Time and fulfilling our different ministries meant we went our separate ways.

Twenty years ago, I found myself in Nairobi at the end of a teaching and training trip and made contact with Clive who was now in Kenya, after seasons in Germany and Sweden. We had opportunity to catch up after not seeing one another for many years. As we shared our experiences, we immediately felt again that joining of hearts. The result was that SOM began to make an impact in Kenya.

We opened schools in various centres. Kisumu, Ruiru, Malindi, Nairobi and Dar-es-Salaam, Tanzania. We also trained Kenyan leaders, notably Peter and Anne Chege, to teach SOM and the work expanded into centres throughout

Kenya that are still functioning through our partnership with Barnabas Ministries.

Jim Palmer, following a successful pastoral ministry of over 50 years found himself in the Philippines on the island of Mindanao, a predominantly Moslem state. He exercised an apostolic ministry linking with leaders and networks of churches. When we made contact after 30 years, he was so impressed with our materials that we began to work together. We saw hundreds of leaders touched, trained and encouraged. Our Asian director now continues this work, and we continue to see it flourish.

We have also been remarkably led by the Spirit in some of our connections; my favourite story is related to the work in Kibera, the massive slum around Nairobi. A church led by Andrew and Ruth Ouma were concerned that leaders they sent for training would not return to the home church but once they had left for Bible College would find other places for their ministry. They decided that the Lord was leading them to set up their own training programme but were aware they did not have any materials.

One of the leadership team was given the task to seek out information. Ruth testifies that she sat in front of her computer with "google search" on the screen and asked the Lord to lead her. The first item to appear in response to her request, was our School of Ministries website. When she read my profile as the director of the work, she says the Lord told her that she should contact this man because this is the ministry they should connect with. I received an email and remarkably I was to be in Nairobi, Kenya, just 2 weeks after our initial contact, and where I would be staying was just a couple of miles from their church. This connection became the beginning of our work in Kibera.

Every place we are involved with has a story of God's leading attached to it. We have many requests for help but walk quietly before the Lord and listen for His voice before engaging in a new school.

Development of School of Ministries

We have seen the work expand into many nations. Some we have visited once or twice others we have been involved with for many years. China, the Philippines, Nepal, Angola, Namibia, Zambia, Rwanda, Zaire, Russia, Albania, Croatia, Belgium, Zimbabwe, Malawi, Nigeria, Jamaica, Australia, USA, and Egypt can all be added to the list of countries we have already mentioned. And recently new nations in West Africa have opened up to us.

Train Teachers

About 4 years ago we felt it was important to train teachers in each of the nation's we were visiting. There was a feeling that we might not always be able to go, that doors might be closed to us, and travel restricted. We had no idea of the impact of Covid at this time.

We began to set about increasing our training activities, particularly in Africa but also in Asia. We upgraded the training programme to make it more compatible for training those in other countries and cultures. Many courses were carried out and numbers of indigenous leaders were trained.

Revision of notes

Around the same time one of the team felt that we should upgrade the notes which had been prepared some 20 years before. They were originally prepared with leaders from the West in mind. At that stage when they were first written, it was not intended that others would teach the materials.

We made the decision to embark on a process of updating, revising, and making the notes more user-friendly bearing in mind that we were asking other leaders to use the notes, as we engaged in training leaders from other nations. As I write that process is almost complete with new notes that enable others to teach our modules in a much more acceptable way.

Reaching Muslims

One of the guys, also about the same time, began to feel a concern about reaching some of the Muslim nations with training. We became aware we were mainly working with countries that would be considered Christian. Our Asian director also responded warmly, so we made this a matter of prayer.

West Africa

We prayed specifically about West Africa and within a short time. Graham, who was our African director at that time visited Liberia. He then connected with a man called Andrew Lendor. He expressed interest in developing training programmes in Africa and so we visited him in Ghana.

A school was held in Kumasi. As a result of the success of this school we then commenced a school in a town called Wa in the north of Ghana. This is a predominantly Moslem town on the border of other Moslem nations.

Within a couple of years, we find ourselves in two centres in Liberia, Sierra Leone, and Guinea with expectations we will soon also be involved in the Gambia and other West African Moslem areas. This has been an exciting phenomenon that God has opened up for the work.

Andrew has become a key "apostolic" figure in the expansion of SOM in West Africa and his on-going involvement has led to us appointing our first indigenous leader in the country. We see this as a fulfilment of the prophesy concerning passing on the baton.[6]

Covid "blessing"

In early March 2019 we held a SOM Conference here in Southampton. We invited and sponsored our key leaders from abroad to visit the UK. We invited our teachers and sponsoring churches in the UK to attend. We had an excellent time of fellowship and vision casting.

Two weeks later Covid broke out and all our plans to travel were curtailed. We had a full programme planned for Africa and Asia. We continued to re-write the modules and along with most churches in the UK began to use social media to communicate.

---

[6] See Chapter 5. Prophetic Direction for School of Ministries.

Within weeks most of us were reasonably competent in video use. WhatsApp, Zoom meetings and Skype became the order of the day. A whole new area of communication opened up to us.

We had previously thought about videoing our School of Ministries modules but because of the time it would take and the exorbitant cost of financing such a venture we had never seriously considered going ahead. Suddenly, with a little help from a professional film maker in the church in Southampton we were able to consider this venture. We had both the time, the capacity and ability to complete this project.

At the time of writing, we have completed 30 of the 35 modules and all the others are in hand to be completed within a few months. This has been a massive team effort and an extraordinary achievement.

During the summer this year, without leaving my home I completed training sessions in around 6 nations, during one month. I was in Malawi completing a training of teachers' programme, and in Uganda, Sierra Leone, Nigeria, Ghana, and Guinea teaching SOM modules. Reaching over 1000 leaders.

This has been an exciting journey with the Lord. During this season many have been referring to Isaiah's prophetic encouragement.

Is. 43:19. Behold, I will do a new thing; now it shall spring forth; shall ye not know it?

We have seen this scripture fulfilled in this season, we perceive that God has used this season in a productive and effective way for School of Ministries. I am reminded of the words of Joseph when he understood that his difficult season had been used by God for purpose.

Gen 45:7: And God sent me before you to preserve for you a remnant in the earth, and to save your lives by a great deliverance.

Seeing Leaders Emerge

Teachers

One of the exciting aspects of this work has been to see men and women emerge as teachers of SOM. I believe the contribution of the UK to the church worldwide is in the realm of our balanced, biblical teaching. Ordinary believers in churches in the UK have a foundation of Bible knowledge and understanding that has hardly been released in the local church but finds an outlet in the developing world where there is a contribution to make. This has meant that considerable numbers of people who are not part of public teaching in their local churches find a place in teaching in Africa and Asia.

We have seen the development of teachers. Katrina is one of those teachers. She has been a faithful servant of the Lord finding a place in the church in serving, mainly in the catering and hospitality realm. Several years ago, inspired by a prophetic challenge she is now involved with SOM and teaching regularly in Africa. She speaks of the revolutionary change that took place in her life as she rose to this challenge. There have been many others.

Students

We can also testify to many individuals who have attended our schools whose lives have been impacted by the teaching and training.

James, Uganda

James had been pastoring a church in southwest Uganda, but a dispute arose in his denomination that led to him losing his church. He was quite broken by the experience but connected with our SOM centre leader who invited him to come on our training programme. James not only received leadership training but was also supported and encouraged to re-establish his heart for church leadership.

Having completed our syllabus over four years and graduated with the diploma, he felt equipped, confident and ready to take up pastoring again and started a church in his home village. The church experienced remarkable growth and twice he had to extend the church building. James has subsequently planted 7 more churches. His life had been transformed by our schools and we saw the fruit of our work.

DK, Orissa, India

We connected with DK, who lives in an isolated part of the very poor state of Orissa. He had several churches and received us warmly. Basil, our Asian director built a strong relationship with DK and within several years the churches were flourishing, growing, and developing. New leaders were emerging, and the work was healthy.

Strong persecution brought a halt to their activities as they were forced to flee their homes and live in the forest. Their only means of communication being mobile phones.

Extraordinary miracles took place. When the batteries of their phones failed, they found a particular leaf of a tree where they rubbed their phones and found them recharging. This went on for about 6 weeks after which they were able to return to their homes.

They had about 37 churches at this time. Within a couple of years, they had established many more churches and numbered 73 centres. This work is still growing and developing with the support of Basil and the SOM teaching programme.

Ruiru, Kenya

One of our first schools was established in Ruiru, Kenya under the leadership of Peter and Ann Chege. They have faithfully hosted a school for over 20 years. They have also trained several other leaders who along with them visit areas in the bush which are difficult for us to reach. They have translated the schools into Kiswahili and seen many leaders emerge in places where we are unable to visit.

At a recent event in Ruiru a school was organised on evangelism. Part of that school was practical and involved going out onto the streets of the town. Over 30 people made a first-time commitment to Jesus on one afternoon because of this activity. An example of the practical nature of the schools.

Bizana, South Africa

The response of the students to the teaching is also very interesting. I was teaching on the person and work of Christ. I was in South Africa in a town in the Eastern Cape. There were approximately 80 leaders attending.

I taught on the work of Jesus during the 3 days He was in the grave. At an appropriate time, I asked if there were any questions. When I have taught on this in the UK, we would have a time of discussion and questions often for a long time. The interpreter touched me on the arm and said, "Before we have questions can we worship?"

It was a fascinating response.

For the next 30 minutes they stood and worshipped Jesus with tears running down their faces in wonder at the work of Jesus on the cross. I was stunned by this response and was challenged to allow the truth about Jesus to travel from my mind to my heart.

Rwashameire, Uganda

Graham Bower reports: After several years of completing School of Ministries in this rural, south-west area of Uganda, it was decided to hold a conference for leaders from the region. Church leaders had never before come together outside of their movements. They had started to develop a small network apart from their denominational settings.

As a result of School of Ministries, they requested we held a conference to bring leaders and their churches together.

Following the SOM around 300 people turned up to the conference.

It was a time of fellowship, building relationships and a man who was blind in one eye received his sight. The result was that these churches began to work together in the region and the following year another conference was held which had an on-going impact.

Seeing it grow

About 5 years ago we were in one of our executive leaders' meetings when Basil asked Graham how many schools, we had carried out that year. Graham said about 36. Basil's response was we should add a nought to that, meaning he thought the Lord was saying this work would expand so that we would be carrying out 360 schools in a year.

As I sat in that room, I wondered in my heart how that could ever be. The step from 36 to 360 is massive. I could not see how that could possibly happen. I must confess I was not in a place of faith for it to happen. However, now I have no doubt that it will come to pass and that we will even exceed that number of schools in the next couple of years as new schools and new nations come online.

Thought to ponder: *How important is it to walk with God, listening for His voice rather than striving in our own strength to make things happen?*

5

PROPHETIC DIRECTION

1 Tim 1:18 "Timothy, my child, I entrust to you this command, which is in accordance with the words of prophecy spoken in the past about you. Use those words as weapons in order to fight well."

1 Tim. 4:14. Do not neglect the spiritual gift within you, which was bestowed on you through prophetic utterance with the laying on of hands by the presbytery.

It is very clear, that Timothy, who at the time Paul was writing was leading the church at Ephesus, had a very clear sense of the prophetic word supporting and establishing him in his ministry.

I believe we should appreciate the importance of the personal, prophetic word. For Irene and me the whole of our lives has been shaped by the prophetic.

Bible College

My first serious prophetic encounter is recounted in Chapter 2: "Call to Ministry".

The impact of that word in changing my father's mind concerning me going to Bible College and the confidence I received that I was hearing from God about the direction for my life brought a sense of assurance, certainty, and clarity that God had called me to serve Him in a particular way.

Walthamstow

It was while we were in Barnet that this sense of prophetic guidance moved to another level. I did not then understand the principle but learnt from experience about the three-fold pathway of prophetic guidance. That God spoke, confirmed, and established his purpose, when he had something to say prophetically that was of significance. I have since formulated a teaching on the subject based on verses in Matthew's gospel:

Matt 18:16. (ISV), 'every word may be confirmed by the testimony of two or three witnesses.'

Amazingly there are at least seven references to this principle in the Bible. I have come to understand that God usually speaks directly to a person, then prophetically confirms that word and finally brings the establishing of that word by the scriptures or through godly leaders. The order is not fixed and often the prophetic will be expressed in a different sequence, but the same three issues will be involved.

We were three years into our leadership of the Barnet church when we attended the opening of a new church building in Walthamstow. Part of that meeting recounted the story of the journey they had been on including a particular scripture in Jeremiah that has been given them at significant times. It was:

"So says the LORD: Behold, I will bring again the captivity of Jacob's tents, and will have mercy on his dwelling places. And the city shall be built on her own hill, and the palace shall remain in its own place." - Jer 30:18.

They had rebuilt the church on the same plot of land increasing its size and quality. I was impressed how that they had been guided so clearly in their building.

Six months later I was in conversation with a friend of mine from that church and he mentioned that the leader of the church in Walthamstow was unwell. As I put the phone down, I heard the Lord say to me clearly, "You are going to Walthamstow".

It was the nearest thing I have heard to the audible voice of God. It was so strong that I looked round to see if anyone was present. I have since concluded that it was a very strong impression in my heart and mind from heaven. I then felt this overwhelming sense of the presence of God. I was about to re-join my wife in our lounge but was so touched by the Holy Spirit that I went into our dining room and there, God's presence reduced me to tears and then joy as if He was affirming the prophetic word, He had spoken to me.

Several days later I visited my brother who lived some 30 miles away. We were in conversation, and he suddenly declared, "I was praying for you yesterday and felt the Lord say to me that you are going to Walthamstow". I had never or since heard him bring a prophetic word of any description, but that confirmation was so clear and distinct. I shared this experience with my wife, Irene, and one other person and then waited upon the Lord.

Nothing happened for months. I prayed over this word and felt that if it was from God, I could trust Him to work it out. One day, as I was reading the scriptures in my usual, daily reading plan, I felt to pause and said to the Lord, "If that word from you concerning Walthamstow is correct, please confirm it."

I then continued to read and was again staggered that the next verse I read was that scripture from Jeremiah that had been so significant in the rebuilding of the church. Previously, I had no idea where it was except that it was in the book of Jeremiah. I was now in no doubt about the prophetic word over us as a family after this three-fold confirmation. We began to plan with our future in mind. We found a leader to replace us in the Barnet church and waited and waited for something to happen.

I reached a point of desperation; I had been offered various other ministry appointments but felt we should wait for the Lord to fulfil His word. It would have been much easier to follow up these other possibilities. Finally, I set a date when I felt it would be irresponsible to wait any longer as I had a family to care for.

On that final day we happened to be visiting a church on the Sunday evening in East Ham. No one was more surprised than I that the leader of the Walthamstow church was present. At the end of the meeting, we went to leave the church; we were part way down the steps from the building when I heard a voice calling me and stopped to respond as I realised it was the leader of that church. He invited us to visit the church two weeks later and within a month we were involved alongside him with a view to taking on the leadership of the church as he planned to step back to retire.

It was a very challenging time, but we learnt that when we were convinced by the three-fold confirmation of prophetic direction we could depend on God to fulfil His Word.

Camp

Whilst we were involved in leadership of the church in Walthamstow God began to stir us again and there came another prophetic interruption to our plans. As I mentioned earlier, we began to realise that we could not lead a church and the camp ministry without someone or something suffering so we began to seek the Lord.

We arrived at the youth camp in August 1978 burdened by this matter and praying for resolution. At the end of the first evening gathering I stayed behind in the chapel and spoke with one of our visiting preachers for that week, a guy called Terry Hanford. He had been involved with us for a few years and I trusted his insight. I shared about this dilemma, and we prayed together. As he began to pray over me, he moved into a prophetic mode and began to quote the following scripture over me.

"No weapon that is formed against you shall prosper; and every tongue that shall rise against you in judgment you shall condemn. This is the heritage of the servants of the LORD, and their righteousness is of me, saith the LORD." - Isaiah 54:17

One of my major concerns had been the reaction to any decision we would make about leaving the church where we had only been for a few years. This verse brought me an immediate encouragement. When Terry finished praying and left the chapel I remained behind and turned to *Isaiah 54* as I had recalled where that verse was found.

I felt prompted to read the whole chapter. It was as if every verse spoke to our situation. Words of challenge about breaking out, words of comfort concerning our children, (I had been concerned about what a move might mean for them if we took this step of faith). Clarity came about so many issues that I wept and surrendered to whatever the Lord had for us. Since that time *Isaiah 54* has been brought to us at various stages on our journey, often in a direct prophetic word.

To take this step meant we were leaving a secure church leadership position with no support, home, or security to follow the Lord. It was a defining moment in our journey. Stories of provision appear in the chapter on the supply of finance and houses from heaven. God had spoken and we responded.

Maidstone Convention

As we were taking this journey, we visited a friend in Kent for a day and discovered there was a conference taking place; the speaker was William Hartley; he was an older man who had been used greatly by God in healing and evangelism over many years in the Pentecostal movement. He preached on a verse from Deuteronomy.

"And He brought us out from there so that He might bring us in to give us the land which He swore to our fathers." - Deut. 6:23.

Remember, we were about to leave our present situation to follow the Lord wherever he might lead us. He spoke of a family who had left everything to pursue the will of God. He gave many examples and testimonies of God working on behalf of those who had taken a step of faith.

There were 300 people in that meeting, but we had one of those unusual encounters with God where every word, every story was relevant to us and our family. Although many may have been blessed and encouraged by this preaching, we knew the Lord was speaking directly to us, I turned to my wife and saw the tears in her eyes. It was an extraordinary prophetic encouragement to take a step of faith.

Leadership Training

Probably the most startling and direct prophetic word came as we were developing a team in Corringham, based on the five ministries outlined in the book of Ephesians.

Eph 4:11,12: "He (Jesus) gave some to be apostles, and some to be prophets, and some to be evangelists, and some to be pastors and teachers, for the perfecting of the saints, for the work of the ministry, for the edifying of the body of Christ.

We had shared with an apostolic leader called Bryn Jones how we felt the Lord was leading us to develop an apostolic team. He invited us to visit him and several of his team in Keighley, Yorkshire.

There were three of us who travelled up to Yorkshire: Mike Godward, Simon Newberry and me. As we had some hours together on the journey in the car, we spoke much of our aspirations and shared what we felt the Lord was saying to us.

It was staggering how our conversation was repeated in the prophetic words we received. As we talked together, I expressed that increasingly I had felt the teaching gift I had begun to exercise needed to expand into teaching and training leaders. During the later years of the youth camp work, I had begun to develop a course for aspiring leaders.

We were also looking to see the church grow leaders in both our own church, and the churches that related to us. I suggested we should commence an evening leadership training programme for our own church and those in the region. There was an immediate response to this from the other guys and we agreed to proceed with this when we returned home.

We arrived in the centre in Keighley and settled in. Within an hour we were gathered together to pray. There were two other prophetic ministries along with Bryn Jones. As we began to pray the guys began to prophesy, they first gathered around Mike Godward.

In the car, on the journey Mike had said, "I cannot teach." The first words spoken over him were, "Do not say I cannot teach, for you will teach but not like other men". The quality and accuracy of the words spoken was amazing.

I still have the written script of the words spoken over me. It was full of encouragement to teach and train. As these guys knew nothing about me it was tremendously inspiring to hear such affirmation. Some of the words that particularly caught my attention were, "You will set your eyes upon young men and women, you will lay your hands upon them and impart your gift of teaching to them as you train them in the Word of God."

Another phrase that has been fulfilled through our international work with School of Ministries was, "All around the nations will be those upon whom you have laid your hands and imparted your gift" It was an extraordinary confirmation of what I felt the Lord was saying to me. He then concluded the word with this phrase, "Your camp will not be a static one". This was strange comment which at that point in time I did not understand but later came to realise its significance.

My understanding of teaching and training at that point of time was that I would require a centre of some kind to work out the vision God was giving me. This never materialised, although we held training in many places, we never had a dedicated centre for training. It is only in hindsight as we developed our training programme across many nations in a multiplicity of centres that I realised the significance of this word, both related to the nations and the camp not being static.

Prophetic Psalmist

It was at another gathering some months later that this word was confirmed in a most exceptional way. I was involved with the organisation of a special event held at the Brentwood International Centre.

We had several well-known speakers at the event and were in the flow of one of the evening gatherings. The worship was very powerful, and I was on the platform as I had to play a part in the evening. I was in the second row directly behind one of our visiting speakers from the USA. He described himself as a prophetic psalmist. He did not know me beyond a brief introduction.

As we were standing worshipping the Lord. He turned around and looked me straight in the eyes. He said, "God has called you as a prophetic teacher to train young men and women for the army of the Lord". He then turned back and continued to worship.

This was a remarkable confirmation of the previous word I had received concerning teaching and training. This left me in no doubt that the direction I had set for my life and ministry was in line with the purposes of God for my life.

I commenced teaching and training immediately in Corringham. Imagine my surprise when we put out a simple brochure advertising our evening training opportunity when 65 people signed up. We thought we might get 25. This led on to further courses and over the next couple of years we held regular evening courses and eventually a full-time one-year course.

From that full-time course, there are those who are still very active in leadership roles in the church around the nation some 35 years later.

Moving to Brentwood increased the breadth of the teaching and training programme. Connecting with the Team Spirit churches brought a new dynamic to the programme, and it expanded. We commenced in Pilgrims Hall, but later moved to the Darash Centre in Brentwood.

The next development of our adventure in teaching and training took place as we moved to Southampton. The prophetic direction we received which is referred to later in this chapter resulted in a full-time course comprising of 36 modules each of 10 hours teaching and a number of courses breaking out from that under the title of "**Deeper** in the Word".

These were all preparation for the development of our School of Ministries International teaching and training programme, now reaching thousands in many nations of the world.

Travelling in Teaching and Training

As we adventured into the realm of teaching and training the Lord continued to speak to us prophetically.

Dale Gentry

During 1991 I was involved in a monthly leader's meeting in Pilgrims Hall. Our friend, Norman Barnes suggested we might like to host a friend of his from the USA called Dale Gentry. We readily agreed to this and so at one of our regular Friday meetings Dale was introduced to us by Norman.

There were some 30 of us sitting in a semi-circle as he addressed us. He brought a message that was fine but nothing spectacular, I believe he had just arrived from the USA that morning and was almost certainly exhausted from overnight travel and jet lag. He then said he would begin to prophesy.

I was sitting at the far end of the left-hand side of the semi-circle, behind where Dale was standing. He began to look for some inspiration as to who to prophecy over and as I sat there, I had this awareness that I was going to be the first one to whom he would bring a word. He turned around looked at me and invited me to sit on the chair directly in front of him. He had a strong southern United States accent and was very loud. He came from a Pentecostal background and spoke loudly in tongues over me for a few minutes. I must confess I was a little uncomfortable.

Then he began to prophesy; he saw me travelling from nation to nation with a suitcase carrying resources. Then he saw me returning and going again from country to country, he completed the word by saying, "You will do it from here."

As I was locked into the prophetic word concerning teaching and training, I did not immediately see how this fitted in with "taking resources from nation to nation". I had not at this time begun to travel in teaching and training and understood "resources" as finance or equipment.

It was a several years before I understood the reference to "resources". We were planning to expand the work of School of Ministries and a special offering was taken to develop the materials for the work. Adrian Thomas, who looked after the finance of the network of churches in Southampton spoke to me and said that he had taken the offering and opened a new account which he had called, "Resources account". A light went on in my head as I realised that this was the interpretation of the prophetic word, very much in line with all that the Lord had previously said. The resources I would be taking from nation to nation were the scriptures.

Interestingly, I visited a conference around the same time and several people brought me a prophetic word. Some of them were well put together and quite complicated. One young guy came up to me and said, almost apologetically, "All I've got is that God will open doors for you to travel".

I arrived home to find my first invitation to travel abroad to teach and train and in the next few months three or four opportunities came for us to travel and we began to see the fulfilment of the prophetic purpose of God.

Southampton

It was around this time that we had begun to build a relationship with Tony Morton. Again, we began to feel a stirring within us and felt the Lord was leading us to re-locate to Southampton.

As we began to pray God began to speak to us. Over a period of 18 months, we received several prophetic indications that the Lord was leading us to Southampton.

This gave me a problem because in the prophetic word from Dale Gentry it had been mentioned that we would fulfil His purpose for us "from here". Originally, I had taken that as the actual building in which we held the meeting, which was a Conference and Retreat Centre called Pilgrims Hall in Brentwood. Based on that I wrote to the trustees of the building and suggested they should give me the property. I received a short and clear note from them that they had not heard that from heaven. I then assumed, that "from here" meant Brentwood. We had acquired a building nearby which had been a training centre and was now the home of New Harvest Community Church as well as being used in our teaching and training programme. Our acquisition of this property had been a wonderful miracle of provision.[7]

However, several more prophetic words came from friends and family all suggesting that God was leading us to Southampton. Our eldest daughter, two prophetic friends, a close colleague, an "Aussie" friend all brought us words that combined to make this leading clear. I was still struggling with this phrase, "from here".

We visited South Africa, the USA and Australia all within a few months in 1995. In South Africa the network we were working with said they wanted to buy us a house to live in so we could serve their churches in teaching and training. We were offered a very attractive proposition in the USA. A good church with a fine building and attractive salary were on offer. Finally, in Australia we were encouraged to return and take on a thriving church at the forefront of what God

---

[7] See Chapter 11. Houses and Cars – Brentwood.

was doing at that time. It was while we were on the flight home to the UK from Australia that I finally came to an understanding that "from here" was speaking of the UK not any particular town. This released us to pursue our sense of prophetic leading.

There then came more prophetic confirmation underlining that the Holy Spirit was active in directing our footsteps. We had made the decision to move to Southampton and were intending to talk with Tony and Hannah Morton at a lunchtime appointment of our thoughts on the matter of relocating to Southampton.

We were holding our annual Springbank Celebration in Brentwood, and the Sunday morning meeting was coming to an end. We were sitting waiting to take Tony and Hannah to our home. As we sat together, one of the speakers at the event, called Rich Hubbard came over to us. He was from another network and knew us by name but knew nothing of our circumstances.

He knelt in front of Irene and I and said, "As I looked at you from across the hall, I felt the Lord say that he wanted you to move to the centre of the Cornerstone network activities, he wants you to move to Southampton for you to work out the vision that He has given you". The timing of that word was amazing and assured us of the will of God for our future.

We began to make our plans.

Carl and Mel Hitt, 1995

We celebrated our 25th wedding anniversary in the Bahamas and in Florida during August 1995. We enjoyed this event around a conference and visiting friends. We found ourselves staying with some friends of ours in Melbourne Beach for a few days.

We heard of a series of special gatherings taking place at the Tabernacle, a well-known church planted by Jamie Buckingham. The churches of the town came together on a Friday evening to wait on the Lord and enjoy times of refreshing that had broken out at that time. We decided to slip into the back of the meeting just for a short time to see what God was doing.

The usual pattern at that time was to invite visitors to stand up and say where they were from. Before I could stop her, as I was not looking to be seen but remain incognito, Irene stood when visitors were asked to make themselves known. I reluctantly joined her and when it was requested, said that we were from London, UK.

There were some 1500 people in the church building that evening. We sat down and enjoyed what was going on. Again, the pattern was to invite testimonies from those who had been touched by the Lord in recent meetings.

We sang another song and the host invited those who had been touched by God to come and make themselves known. At the end of the song the leader of the meeting stood up and declared that this had never happened before in this series of meetings but that no one had come to bring a testimony.

He then said, it would be good to hear about what is going on in the UK. Where are that couple from London? Now we found ourselves addressing this congregation and sharing what was happening in various parts of the nation. We then went back to our seats. So much for my desire to be anonymous.

There were visiting speakers that evening from Washington. Their names were Carl and Mel Hitt. Carl began to share but mentioned that his wife Mel had a few prophetic words before he preached. Her first words were, "Where is that couple from London?" We were on our feet again. She began her prophetic encouragement with the words, "You are moving to a new location. From there God is going to fire you out into the nations. You will be like arrows fired from a bow, but the arrows will be tied to a tether (rope), and you will be fired and then gathered back in. You will be fired to Africa, India, the USA, Jamaica, Brazil and other nations." Having just three months before made the decision to move to Southampton this was another helpful directional prophecy that confirmed the correctness of our move, and of our call to teach, train and travel.

There was also a very personal encounter for Irene concerning this move. Three of our children were living in the same town as us in Essex at that time, and one daughter lived in London. Irene was quite upset at the prospect of living so far away from them.

In the September of that year, we attended the annual leader's conference in Southampton. Keith Hazell was a recognised prophetic ministry and was involved in the programme. We had made contact and become friends but at that time he knew nothing of our plans. As he was about to pass Irene in a corridor of the building he stopped and said to her that it was right for us move to this region and that she would have her family around her.

When we returned home, we shared our plans with our four children. Three of them were married and one had children. They all affirmed the rightness of our move and three of them said they wanted to move with us, to be near us. The one daughter in London did not move at that time but since has come to live in the area and is now in leadership of one the local churches.

There was no doubt about where we should live and be involved in ministry.

Prophetic Direction for School of Ministries

As a result of the demise of the programme in the UK and subsequent conversations I was feeling quite low and tired, and said to the Lord, "I have had enough and am ready to give up, I will go and be a taxi driver". I was in my early 60's and wondered whether this was the time to step back.

At that time, we visited India and in the Sunday morning meeting Basil, the leader of the church, called Irene and I forward. He said that early that morning he had received an open vision, meaning he saw this scene with his eyes open. He reported that the presence of God had filled his prayer room, and that he saw me on a racetrack, running with a baton looking around for someone to pass it on to. He said: "The baton changed into 7 batons and as I came around the bend of the racetrack, I saw 7 people ready to take those batons and run with them."

He asked the Lord what the 7 batons represented, and the Lord said, "The 7 continents of the world". He then saw the scene rewind and play again, this time there were many batons and many runners waiting to receive them. When he asked what this meant, he felt the Lord say, "The many nations in those continents".

He then went on to say that I should not say, "It is time to give up". These were the exact words I had used when in my own prayer room with nobody present. I began to weep. He then went on to prophesy over Irene and I of the Lord's hand upon our lives and of the development and expansion of SOM alongside some personal words.

It was one of those significant occasions, when the tears flowed freely and the sense of the presence of God overwhelmed us. Since that moment, we have taken that word about the passing on of the "baton" as a strategic word from the Lord concerning the future of the ministry. It has been a source of joy seeing key ministries picking up various batons and running with them!

Several weeks later we were visiting our friends, Andrew and Kay Gill for lunch. At the conclusion of lunch Andrew returned to his work and as we were about to leave Kay said, "Please wait a little while I feel I have a word from the Lord for you."

She left the room and returned with a quiver of arrows. My mind went immediately to the word from Mel Hitt concerning us being fired like arrows into the nations. Kay knew nothing of this. She then went on to describe how she saw the word of God being fired like arrows through the ministry of School of Ministries. Again, we were astounded and humbled at the significance of this word for the future of this work.

Even now at this late stage in our journey God is still encouraging us with the prophetic word. Just recently we have received three prophetic words from three different people, in three different contexts encouraging us to speak into the lives of the next generation to inspire them to become all that God intends them to be.

I do not know why we have received so much prophetic direction and guidance in our lives; it may be a sign of weakness that we need such constant encouragement from the Lord because of our insecurity. All I do know is that it has been very important for us to keep our ears open for the voice of God through the prophetic in all its forms.

Thought to ponder: *What prophetic direction have I received. Is it being fulfilled?*

6

CAMP – FROM SMALL BEGINNINGS

Eph 2:10 "For we are his workmanship, created in Christ Jesus for good works, which God prepared beforehand, that we should walk in them."

Irene and I for many years led youth camps in Sussex; they operated under the title of Sussex Pentecostal Youth Camps. This work was commenced by a group of church leaders from North London first running a youth camp in Hastings, Kent in 1971. I was one of that original team.

By 1973 I took on full responsibility for this work, and we had acquired the use of a school called Great Walstead in Lindfield, Sussex. Until 1987 my wife and I led this work along with a great team of people who volunteered to work with us. Many became close friends as well as colleagues. In 1975 we also pioneered a camp in a school nearby called Ashdown House which was near East Grinstead in Sussex.

We ran these schools in parallel. Chas Musgrave worked

alongside us and administrated that school. We worked as a team hosting some 350 young people each week for 4 weeks during August. We also commenced two further schools in Farney Close School, Bolney, and Shoreham school, which was a camp for children.

Over those years we reached thousands of young people between the ages of 11-18 as well as many older young people attending, some as leaders of their youth groups.

We saw 1000s of young people come into a relationship with Jesus through salvation, 100s of young people filled with the Holy Spirit, many begin to exercise the gifts of the Spirit as well as dozens of young people receiving a call to ministry. Many of those who responded to the challenge to surrender their lives to Jesus are in church leadership today.

Just recently, at a national conference, while listening to a leader of a large church in the Midlands, I realised I recognised his name. I made contact and he stated that he had visited our camps over several years as a teenager and first encountered the Lord at Great Walstead in our camp meetings.

We are constantly hearing stories and meeting people who met Jesus over this period at these camps. I know we can sometimes view past events through "rose tinted" spectacles but I believe we touched something really significant of the presence and power of God at those times. Those days are among the most effective and fruitful I have experienced in my life and ministry.

Bryn Eirias

I mentioned our own experiences as young people at the holiday centre we regularly visited in North Wales. I believe we saw something of the potential of this ministry and its effectiveness which is why we so readily became involved in the young camps in the early 1970's.

When we went to Bible College it was our intention to work in the centre when we completed our studies in the summer of 1970, following our marriage. However, while we were at college the centre was sold due to a compulsory purchase to make way for a major road. This ended any thoughts on that matter, but God had put something in our hearts that we wanted others to experience.

It is fascinating how Irene's career path prepared her for the running of the practical side of a camp with skills in planning, catering, and caring for a large group of people, which she acquired in her children's work ministry. My administrative and accounting abilities also were a positive contribution to the work. Again, this sense of God working in our lives and arranging for us to acquire the necessary skills is an indication of "His providence".

Small beginnings

We commenced with a school in Hastings in 1971, moved on to another school in Chelsfield, Kent and another in Yeovil before commencing using the school in Great Walstead in 1973. Those early years brought challenges. There were some break downs in relationships; we faced some doctrinal issues; there were also financial challenges; alongside the back breaking work of running such an event.

We finally began to establish the work with a brilliant team, mainly people from the Walthamstow church and later many from the Corringham fellowship. We would be thoroughly exhausted by the end of August and always planned a week for a break following such effort. Like every effective and fruitful project there is a price to pay to see the end result. Our children thoroughly enjoyed the camps, even though it took up their summer break from school. It was a highlight for them over the years.

When we felt it was time to hand over the work, we were conscious that we had not been able to take holidays as a "normal" family would, so we arranged to take our kids to Disney world in Orlando, Florida. We had an excellent time; it was brilliant; it cost a considerable amount of money. When we returned home one of our daughters said, "We have had a great time, but we would rather have gone to camp!".

Towards the end of the 1980's we found ourselves in a time of change, we were getting older and as we approached our 40's found the running of the camps quite difficult. In 1986 we had our usual planning meeting and made the necessary arrangements to go ahead for the next year, 1987.

In our local church there was a guy called Fred. He had been part of the camp work and he came to me a couple of weeks after the planning meeting and said that as he had prayed, he felt the Lord was calling us to consider whether we should go ahead for the next Summer. He was a guy with some prophetic history, but I immediately said that we had already made the decision to go ahead and could not consider his suggestion concerning not running the camps for the next year.

I regret my off-hand treatment of that conversation as the camp of 1987 although on the surface was successful was the most difficult time for us. We did not fill the camps for the first time. This meant that for the first time in our history we ran at a loss. Irene suffered with health problems for the whole 4 weeks, particularly struggling with a back issue. I had some really difficult situations that arose during the camp and found myself repenting for not taking notice of the prophetic challenge presented to us. By the end of that camp, we knew it was time for us to move on into the next phase of our ministry.

During the last few years of running the camp work I had begun to take a small group of the older youth during the morning Bible study sessions. I had prayed and invited young people who I saw the hand of God on to be part of that group and began to encourage them with teaching and training on leadership. This proved to be very fruitful and there are many leaders of churches today who were part of those sessions. This was part of the journey that led us into the next stage of our ministry.

Thought to ponder: *If this kind of ministry is so effective, what aspects of it am I or my church involved?*

7

CAMP – STORIES

Ps. 145:4,5. "One generation shall praise Your works to another and shall declare Your mighty acts. I will speak of the glorious honour of Your majesty, and of Your wonderful works.

Before we move on, I would like to dwell on the youth camp work a little and tell some of the stories of people whose lives were impacted through this ministry. There are those who suggest that many of the young people just have an emotional experience at such events and that may be true for some, but we could write a book on the stories of those who had a transforming encounter with God that changed their lives.

The Sussex Phenomena

One of my friends suggested we should call this account of the work of the youth camps, "The Sussex Phenomena" such was the impact of the work. There are many stories we could tell, here are just a few of them:

The Transformative Nature of Christian Camps - Revd Dr Mark Griffiths JP

I grew up in a Welsh mining valley. I was 15 before I set foot in a church building. God was nothing more than an abstract concept who may or may not be real. I didn't care one way or the other, I was completely uninterested. It was in my Welsh valley on a wet Friday evening that I eventually went to church. It was a youth group in a small Pentecostal Chapel with a corrugated iron roof.

I had gone because I liked a girl who attended, she had invited me, but I quickly made a lot of other friends. There were songs on a guitar, testimonies, prayers and preaching. It was several months later that I attended a Sunday Service and that really was something else.

The place was packed (although anything over 40 meant it was packed) and everyone seemed to own a tambourine with ribbons. It was certainly lively. And just before my sixteenth birthday I decided to become a follower of Jesus and was baptised in the local Baptist church. But there was no real certainty and certainly, no Damascus Road spectacular event.

Several months later a man came to speak at our church who had a recognised prophetic gift. He called me to the front and said these words, "God will take away your spirit of a doubting Thomas and place within you a spirit of adventure."

At that point I had never left the valley. But the prophetic word changed me. I had a new spirit but no money! So, at the age of 16, to my parent's surprise, I wrote to several youth camps to ask if I could come and help out. There were quite a few to choose from at that point. Many wrote back and said they recruited from the churches they were in relationship with, a Scottish camp (I really did apply everywhere) wrote back to say I would be younger than most of the people attending! But Peter Butt wrote back from Sussex Pentecostal Youth Camps and offered me a place, for four weeks. I wasn't completely sure where Sussex was. Nevertheless, a few months later I caught a bus to London and another to Haywards Heath and then walked the final 3 miles to Great Walstead School.

In week 1 - I washed dishes, thousands of dishes. In week 2 - I washed pots and pans, week 3 saw me promoted to tuck shop and smoothie bar, but I landed again in pots and pans for week 4 which was a family week. It did feel strange being on staff when many of the young people attending were older than me. They came from all over the country, places I had never heard of.

I shared a dorm with some older teens from Dudley – their accents made me smile, but at least they were understood. Not many people could understand my thick Welsh Valley accent. I still keep in touch with some of them today, one of them is a vicar in Ireland.

Every day started with staff prayer, we worshipped together, prayed for each other, and prophesied over one another. There was a short exhortation from the Bible. By week two I was asked to deliver that exhortation. It was the first time I shared outside of my local church, and I had only shared there once. Then the teenagers would fill the dining hall for breakfast, we would wash up and then join them for their morning seminars.

Incredible worship, hundreds of teenagers with their hands held high worshipping Jesus. Then activities and lunch and more activities and dinner and an evening gathering. More incredible worship, God moving by His Spirit in a way I had never experienced before. I was prayed for on numerous occasions, learning to minister as the Spirit led. The speakers were men like David Shearman, Gerald Coates, Ian Green and of course Peter Butt who ran the camps – not many female speakers in those days.

Such intense worship, forming so many important friendships that continued. These were the days of letter writing and I sent and received dozens. And of course, day trips to Littlehampton and late-night bonfires and barbecues and late-night walks and at the end of the week, prize giving! I won best Welsh person most weeks – mainly on account of being the only Welsh person.

These were among the best experiences of my teenage years. I did this for two years before moving to help the Assemblies of God Youth Council with their camp in Llandovery, mid-Wales and then a year later they took over the running of the Sussex camps so back to Great Walstead, which for me felt like coming home. I would continue washing dishes, cleaning pots and pans, but I would also add extra skills… cleaning toilets, running sports activities, mopping floors, before becoming one of the speakers eventually leading my own camps.

But it was in that very first camp in Sussex that I clearly heard God calling me to full time ministry. I know this happens to many people. The intensity of camp is the perfect place to hear God. But I had only been a Christian a year and had no Christian background.

Three years after that first camp I went to Theological College, a place called Mattersey Hall, and three years after that I took my first job as a Children's Pastor in Milton Keynes. I've been employed by churches of varying denominations ever since, doing jobs from senior minister all the way up to children's pastor!

I've ministered for churches in Milton Keynes, Bletchley, Nottingham, Slough and Bracknell. Was Head of Children and Family Ministry for New Wine, have published 10 books, been involved in camps all over the world and am now head of Missiological Research for the Church in Wales, combined with holding responsibility for curate training and the development of children, young people and family ministry across Wales.

I recently also agreed to join the Scripture Union National Council – partly because I believe in the power of camps. I have now been working for churches for 30 years. Not bad for a Welsh Valley boy who hadn't been out of Wales until he was 16.

But none of this was my doing - not really. My life came into focus at the Sussex Pentecostal Youth Camps many decades ago. I owe so much to those camps and the prayerful men and women of God who made them happen. But they also show how transformative such experiences are for young people. For me it was life changing.

Stephen Hyde

"It is impossible to put a value of what Youth camp in Sussex did for me personally. The first year I attended at just the tender age of 12, I won a prize for pain of the week.

Yet it is not that I will remember, but rather the Wednesday night when I ran to the front of the chapel, constrained by the Holy Spirit to give my life to Christ. Instantly, I began to speak in tongues.

The following 7 or 8 years just built on that initial experience, and a deep hunger for the things of the Spirit grew in me. It became an annual pilgrimage. As a result, some of my friends came to Christ and then would join me for this the annual trip down South. Early morning prayer meetings, and teachings stirred my soul, amazing worship and preaching in the evening services built more desire and hunger for God. It was in the chapel at camp, I prophesied for the first time, moved out in words of knowledge and without fear prayed for others to be filled with the Spirit.

At the age of fifteen I received a prophetic word during an evening service, and I knew God had called me into the ministry. Camp remains for me the high-water mark of intense spiritual encounters with God.

I am now married with three sons and am leading a thriving church in the West Midlands. I will be eternally grateful for camp. Happy memories, but also times of encounter that have shaped my life and ministry. It was in that place, I launched out and glimpsed what God had for me. I caught a vision for more of God."

Robert

Several years ago, I visited the church that Stephen Hyde now leads. On that occasion an older lady came up to me and said, "You do not know me, but I know who you are, and am so grateful to God for you."

I was intrigued by this statement and then she told me her story. Her son Robert at the age of 13 was in serious trouble. He had been excluded from school, was in trouble with the police and completely hostile and rebellious in the home. In desperation, she and her husband had agreed for him to go with Stephen to the youth camp, hoping that they would get a break from the trouble he was causing. He came to our camp and met Jesus who transformed his life.

Upon returning home he walked through the door of his home and to his parent's utter amazement declared that he had found the Lord Jesus as His Saviour and Lord and that his life had been changed. Such was the change in this 13 years old boy that his mother visited the church with him the next Sunday and herself made a commitment to follow Jesus.

She was followed the next Sunday by Robert's sister and although the husband held out for a few weeks he too had responded to the gospel and was now in relationship with the Lord. She wept as she told me the story of how her whole family had found the Lord because of camp, and I joined her. It took 30 years to hear that story, I wonder how many other stories there are like that from those days.

Robb and Sally Harman

"Walstead Youth Camp under the leadership of Peter and Irene Butt inspired me and shaped my thinking about what Church could look like. 40 years ago, during my summer seasons in West Sussex I saw Church as deeply spiritual, relational and fun. 'Why can't life be like this all the time?

That's what we wanted; the key elements woven into our "normal' lives. During summer camp we were discipled to have quality 'quiet times' as well as attending the staff reflection times and evening meetings. Peter particularly encouraged us to take personal responsibility for our walk with God.

The main meetings were full of Holy Spirit power and some meetings have stayed with me like they were yesterday. For example, David Shearman spoke one night on 'rise up like eagles' a truly amazing moment, David left us open to God's heart for us and the world around us.

We as Church were focused on Jesus and him only. We as Church built relationships with others. In the girls' dorm, in the kitchen at the 3 times a day meal times we lived alongside one another. Young people from around the country hanging out together sharing 'God moments' dreaming big for the Church.

We had to learn to how to get along, we started work early in the kitchen, working together. I am sure I was the messiest teenager back at the dorm. We built fantastic friendships and met people of all ages around the table. Hospitality and the discipline of eating together were modelled well at Walstead. I really took that on board and as a leader in the local 24-7 Prayer Community.

We as Church now meet intentionally around the table to eat with friends some of whom are of faith and others who are just hungry. Fun - camp was fun. Church should be fun; it can be a celebration of life together with God. We learnt to serve in practical ways with love alongside friends' day by day. Of course, it was fun!"

Suzanne Matthams

I know for me personally camp had an impact on my life in many different ways. I have fond memories of long summers being with my friends: likeminded people. Summers were about being able to withdraw from the pressures of school and college and be in an environment in which I felt I belonged.

That said, it was also a place of challenge, having to work alongside others, work long hours and do work you weren't used to doing, it was certainly character building. It was also a place to develop and grow in ministry. I am thankful that I was given the opportunity to be part of the children's camps in particular as this helped shape my desire to make working with children my career and full-time ministry.

When I moved to Hampshire 12 years ago and joined Newlife Church, the youth work was established, and a February half-term camp and a summer camp were already part of the church diary.

My experience of youth camp ensured I was fully committed to encouraging my four children to be part of the camp experience. The exciting thing for me is that the 'camp legacy' has lived on through my children. My eldest daughter and her husband are the youth pastors at our church, and the vision for youth camps is as vibrant as ever. We had 180 young people on camp this summer all from our church and the local schools.

I think there is something special about coming away and setting aside a designated time to minister to young people.

It is purposeful and intentional. There is so much that distracts and pulls at our young people. Being together all in one place over a set period quietens those distractions. I also think that camp life builds that sense of belonging, young people can feel a connection to others who are like them.

One of the things I also remember for myself was that it was a place where people had time for me. I had many encounters with God through spending time and being ministered to by other individuals. Young people need attention - camp is a place where they get it. It is often at the times you least expect it when you are having a conversation with a young person and God just shows up and brings healing, revelation and impacts that young person's life.

I remember the prayer and preparation long before the event, our whole church was behind and involved in camp. There was great preaching of the truth - no compromising. Young people do not need a watered-down message, they need the radical message of the gospel. I remember teams of workers who caught the vision and heart of the camp and got involved. Sharing the vision of what is it God wants to say and do. Unity of heart and vision among the team. Listening to the young people to see what kind of programme they want and what is relevant to them. It is easy to put a programme together based on what the leaders think will work rather than listening to what the young people are into. Youth workers involvement was also essential, them having a clear role.

Remarkably in all the business of life at camp and in all the excitement, I know for me I learned to spend time alone with Jesus and to cultivate that personal relationship with Him.

It was a time that God spoke deeply into my life either through the teaching, prophetic words, prayer ministry or talking with others. I made decisions that would affect the course of my life whilst at camp: which university to go to, who to marry and what career I should go into.

Camps were part of my foundation for the tough times on my journey. It has been the teaching and the foundations from my youth that have stood me in good stead. Thank you for camp - it's part of my DNA

Chris and Usha Scott

"Ahh…. those long summer days at Great Walstead School back in the late 70's and early 80's. What special times they were, and still today they invoke very vivid and fond memories for me and the Hounslow Young Peoples Group as we experienced them together.

I look back on my years at youth camp with such thankfulness and joy, and I know without a shadow of doubt that they had a profound impact on my spiritual journey in Christ. I loved the whole atmosphere of camp; the fun, the sport, and the nocturnal antics (less said the better), but what was perhaps most extraordinary was the deep and powerful sense of God's presence every night in the meetings.

As a teenager and a relatively young Christian at the time, those times of worship, preaching and ministry were deeply formational for me. They cemented my relationship with Jesus, and my conviction to serve him with my life.

One of the most memorable moments for me was when I was baptised with the Holy Spirit one evening during a preach by David Shearman. I had been seeking the Holy Spirit for a long while but hadn't experienced him fully until that point. Right in the middle of his preach David just stopped and told everyone to turn to the person next to them and pray for whatever it was they wanted or needed from God. My mate was next to me, and he prayed for me to receive the Holy Spirit and that was it! Instantly I was filled with the Spirit and began to speak in tongues for the first time. That was truly a breakthrough experience for me, and I believe it propelled me on to a life of ministry and service that I am still passionate about 40 years on.

For me and my wife Usha, we are so privileged to have experienced those amazing years at camp, and even more so, to have stayed in close relationship with Peter and Irene over the last 40 years. What's more, those youth camps really got into our blood!

When we had kids of our own, we served for years in camp ministry too, and made sure they experienced it in the same way we did. So, for myself and for the countless others whose lives were shaped and moulded by those wonderful camp experiences at Great Walstead, we are deeply thankful to the Lord for Peter and Irene, and for all those who passionately served with them as part of their teams over those years. The extraordinary impact and the lasting legacy of their camp ministry is truly exceptional, and still being felt around the world today; and long may it continue."

Nic and Debbie Hughes.

"Spending a week – or more, if you were really serious – at the summer camps that Peter and Irene ran, have become simply unforgettable experiences for us, and their impact has left a legacy not only in our lives but have positively impacted the lives of our children too.

The youth group from Hounslow Pentecostal Church started attending in the late 70's, with anything from 40 to 60 young people coming back each year. Days always seem to be sunny; sports were seen as a vital ingredient to the programme – I remember one year, our youth group entering teams in the 5-aside football ranging from Hounslow A to Hounslow G just to accommodate everyone.

I remember busking in Haywards Heath, asking the locals if they had seen 'George's bottom set' and being genuinely anxious that if we didn't tow the line, Patsy White would really BOOT us!

But, by far and away THE most important and lasting impact on our lives personally, were the incredible times in the presence of God during the worship services and the prayer meetings. It was here that we cultivated the discipline and joy of praying passionately and corporately.

Being in the atmosphere of worship cultivated in Debbie and me the hunger and the understanding of what it means to pursue God in worship. It was at camp that I began to develop as a worship leader and musician; that both Debbie and I were exposed to the prophetic and were called into ministry – independently of each other; we were encouraged and given space to move in the gifts of the spirit and experienced what it meant to wait upon God; where we were taught what Biblical leadership looks like and where we were recognised as being set apart for service in the Kingdom by other Godly leaders whom we came to hugely respect and love.

The legacy means that today, Debbie and I serve as ministers leading a church in South London. We had the privilege of hosting camps in our own right and our children grew up in the same kind of environment which has equally left an indelible mark of the kingdom upon their lives.

We are so grateful to all those who gave up so much of their time and energy to pour into our lives. Words are simply not enough to demonstrate how truly thankful we are, but we hope that our lives are a testament to the investment that people made into us in such formative years of our spiritual development."

Sound Bites

David and Glennis Hyde: "We frequently talk of camp days with fondness and thankfulness. In our opinion it was effective and fruitful. Not only did camp have a great spiritual input on our three children - it had a great input on us too as we served on the staff for one three week period. We thank God for you and the camps being an important figure in our children's spiritual development."

Billy Ritchie: (Leadership team of Milton Keynes Christian Centre). "Almost every significant spiritual experience in my teens took place at Sussex Camps. My very first year there was when I decided to stop playing games with God, it was also my first experience of the power of the Holy Spirit in my life and lastly it was where God called me into ministry."

Frank and Julie Hodge: Frank was a rebellious mid-teen from a Christian family in Liverpool. A group from the church his family attended came to one of our early camps in the Bristol area. He said he does not know why he came. He had nothing else to do so thought he would come along.

The first evening God spoke directly to him, and he surrendered his life to Jesus. During the Tuesday morning prayer gathering we prayed for those who had a desire to be filled with the Spirit. Frank was sitting in a window seat, and I went over to pray with him. As I laid hands on him, he began to sing in the language of the Spirit. The tongues that flowed from his lips were beautiful, melodious and inspired.

As Frank began to grow and develop in his life with the Lord so did his gift in music. He has become a key-board player of some distinction and a prophetic psalmist often declaring the word of the Lord through prophetic song. Frank was a regular at youth camp over many years, he met Julie who became his wife, and together they have served God for many years.

Graham Blake: I started going to Great Walstead youth camp as a 13-year-old with my church youth group. For the next six years I had numerous encounters with God during those times at camp. At 15 years old I felt the call of God one evening into full-time ministry. I could take you to the seat in that chapel where I was sitting. David Shearman was speaking that night, and he said there are young men and women called into full-time leadership and you know who you are. It was if I was the only person in the room, as I sat, I began to literally cry. It was an evening that changed my life and of course my future. At the age of 17 I began to serve as a volunteer on staff and it was at the age of 18, I met my wife, Michele. We are still happily married and serving God in leadership in Norfolk. Those days were life changing moments that have led us to much of what we are doing today.

Susanne Singh (daughter of Peter and Irene Butt): When I think about Sussex youth camps, I remember my youth. From an early age right up until I was 16 my summers were filled with the fun and adventure of meeting young people from across the UK. It was in this environment that I encountered God in a deep and meaningful way.

I was influenced by those who came to speak and experienced God's presence in a way that inspired, challenged and shaped my journey in Jesus. I was filled with the Holy Spirit alongside other children and young people, and we dared to take risks in the prophetic, ministered to one another and trusted that God had a purpose for our lives. I know that I am the woman I am today because of what God did over those summers.

Call to Ministry

There are many others who can testify to camp being the source of the call of God to them. I distinctly remember one evening when three young men surrendered their lives to God, recognising the call of God to leadership. I had preached on those significant verses written by Paul to the Philippians

Phil 3:7-10 "But what things were gain to me, those I counted loss for Christ. Yea doubtless, and I count all things but loss for the excellency of the knowledge of Christ Jesus my Lord: for whom I have suffered the loss of all things, and do count them but dung, that I may win Christ, And be found in him, not having mine own righteousness, which is of the law, but that which is through the faith of Christ, the righteousness which is of God by faith: That I may know him, and the power of his resurrection, and the fellowship of his sufferings, being made conformable unto his death".

I felt a strong urge to appeal for those who felt that God was calling them to leadership in the church. I felt I had a word of knowledge about their struggles to make that commitment but encouraged them to respond to the call of God upon their lives. I was not expecting a great number to respond and was not surprised when only three guys stood up. They were Stephen Page, Simon Newberry and Paul Chamberlain. All three had been leaders of youth groups and had begun to reveal leadership qualities.

Within a couple of years, Stephen had planted a church in Feltham which grew significantly, he recently stepped back from leading a successful, growing church in South London. Paul Chamberlain successful pioneered a new church that grew to several hundred members. Simon pastored in Diss, then became part of a leadership team in Corringham before returning to Diss to pioneer a missions work in Kisumu, Kenya. I mention those stories as I believe they can be replicated over and over.

Partners for life

Several young people who visited camp also found their life partner. Although we discouraged courting that involved any kissing and cuddling, camp was a place where many relationships were formed that later resulted in marriage. Frank and Julie, John and Glenda, Graham and Michelle, Paul and Joanne are just a few of the names that come to mind. As far as I am aware, the relationships that led to marriage at camp have produced strong, stable, and lasting partnerships that exist to this day.

Thought to ponder: *Meditate on encounters you have had with God and their effect.*

8

CAMP – CHURCHES IMPACTED

Phil. 1:3 "I thank my God upon every remembrance of you".

We also saw radical changes in youth groups that impacted the local church they came from.

Walthamstow

In the early days of the camps the Walthamstow church was a source of great support. Senior team leaders made up the executive group that drove this work and an army of volunteer staff supported the work. Chas and Chris, Margaret and Mike, John and Rita, Ted and Rose are just a few of the key people who came together to make this ministry so effective. Many of them gave of their time sacrificially.

Then there were those who came and worked hard in various activities, many of those who were involved were also impacted by their encounters with the Lord, as was the church. There are still couples in the church who met the Lord at those camps.

The Scottish Invasion

One of the most memorable weeks at camp was when a coach load of young people descended on Great Walstead from the North-East of Scotland. The leader of that group, Roger Blackmore writes:

"I arrived in the remote northeast corner of Scotland in the summer of 1976 at the ripe old age of 26. I had been invited to pastor the well-established Assemblies of God Church in Cairnbulg, a small fishing community 40 miles north of Aberdeen.

One of the reasons they wanted such a young pastor was that they were in a desperate battle to hold onto the next generation, many of whom were growing up with little interest in continuing to pursue the faith of their parents. Developing a relevant and effective youth program was one of my top priorities – but it was a tough task.

When my good friend Peter Butt invited me to speak at the Sussex Pentecostal Youth Camp at Great Walstead School in August of the following year, I felt this would be an excellent opportunity to get some of these teenagers away into a different environment for a while, spend time building relationships with them and expose them to whatever God might do that week.

It didn't start well. The coach trip from one end of the country to the other took us over 26 hours, which was a long time for a group of around 40, comprising young people from our own church and from Fraserburgh Assembly of God. Hot, tired, they arrived full of complaints and were certainly far from ideal campers those first few days.

We had some wonderful evening services in the school chapel over the weekend. I was paired up with Ken Williams from Poole and we were the preaching team. Ken did a fantastic job, and I did okay too, but our kids appeared unmoved by it all.

After Monday night's activities were over, I went back to my room and started to pray specifically for our group. And then I prayed God would help me, because I wasn't getting through to them. I needed something extra myself in that situation. In my desperation, I read these words from the Bible over and over again –

1 Chronicles 4:10 (KJV) - And Jabez called on the God of Israel, saying, Oh that thou wouldest bless me indeed, and enlarge my coast, and that thine hand might be with me, and that thou wouldest keep me from evil, that it may not grieve me! And God granted him that which he requested.

As I read them, I began to weep, asking God to enlarge my coast – take me deeper in my own relationship with him. Then I prayed the same for our Scottish teens. I prayed well into the night.

The following evening it was my turn to preach to the youth groups from different parts of the country who were there that week. I spoke on the prayer of Jabez and when I finished, I invited anyone who wanted to have a relationship with God or to deepen their relationship with God to come forward for prayer. A few responded, nothing remarkable, and then it was as if the floodgates opened and from all over the chapel young people started coming forward, many in tears. That became a night of huge spiritual breakthrough, including virtually all of the 40 teens from north of the border.

If the story ended there, it would be a good one, but it didn't and it got even better. Because once camp was over, it was a totally transformed busload of passengers who made the long journey home. Now they were singing worship songs they had learned that week, excitedly talking about all that had happened and eager to be in church the following morning. And they were.

Their newfound faith and enthusiastic worship made it obvious that God had done something revolutionary in their lives. That energy injected fresh life and purpose into the whole church. A few weeks later Peter Butt and I baptized many of these young people in the North Sea and over 40 years later time has shown that this was not some seven-day camp experience that fizzled out in the weeks that followed, but a turning point that has shaped the entire lives of those involved, most of whom continue to serve God faithfully to this day and several of whom have spent their lives in full time Christian ministry.

Sussex Pentecostal Youth Camp made a huge impact on a generation in the northeast of Scotland – and on me."

Corringham

As the camps developed and Irene and I re-located to Corringham in Essex the focus of the work also changed and the local church in Essex became a place where numbers of young people and even older folks became involved.

We experienced a move of the Holy Spirit in Thurrock and worship was one of the major pillars of that work. This overflowed into the youth camp work and our camp meetings became a place where many experienced a new freedom in their worship.

I remember specifically one year when a few in the church had begun to dance a little, but only a few were really free in this area, and they were mainly the leaders. A group of around 30 attended the camp and broke free in worship.

I remember the first Sunday back in the local church when the young people all began to dance freely at the front of the building. It became a breakthrough moment for the church in their worship. The older young people at the church became regulars at the camps, many finding ways to spend all four weeks involved with the work. The special relationship that developed as we worked together to see God move still exists today. There is a bond of mutual friendship and fellowship that was first created as we worked together in the camps.

Thought to ponder: *Should I be encouraging my leaders to embrace this ministry and make it part of our church life?*

9

CAMP – ITS IMPACT AND EFFECTIVENESS

2 Cor 3:2. "You are our epistle written in our hearts, known and read by all men"

It is reasonable to ask the question. "Why is youth camp ministry so effective and fruitful?" Ric Joyner of Morning Star Ministries, Charlotte, North Carolina, USA, recently made this statement. "Research has shown that as many as 90% of all new believers come to the Lord before age 18, and over 80% of those come through Christian camps". If this is correct, I would like to evaluate this ministry, understand why this is so, and seek to answer the question.

David Lakin

One of my good friends, who I first met at the holiday centre in North Wales, and later turned up at the same Bible College is a guy called Dave Lakin.

He originally hails from Wombwell in Yorkshire and has an amazing gift and ability working with children and young people. For many years he hosted a children's camp ministry in the peak district called, Bonsall Camp. Hundreds of children owe their first encounter with Jesus and their first steps in their Christian life to encounters with God at this place. Dave then began to be more involved in youth camp work alongside his church leadership role. He makes this comment about the value of this ministry.

"Camp was effective for the following reasons: Each Youth group that came to camp became aware that there are many more young people who are Christians in other parts of the country; It was a place where friendship and courtship developed, and great marriages resulted.

There were no distractions, they heard the Word of God every day from men who knew how to communicate with young people. This was a 'Life Changing' week for hundreds who came every year. One sensed that upon each camp, the key was the anointing of the Holy Spirit. Today, there are many in the Ministry who came away from camp, having received the Call of God upon their lives. One Man that stands out is Daniel. He came to camp a sinner and returned a saint. Daniel is now a Youth Pastor.

This year was my twenty second year of running Youth and Children's Camps. Why do I keep going? Because it is a place where God turns up every year, many make first time decisions to follow Jesus, many older young people and leaders of youth groups get closer to God."

Keys to effectiveness

My own observations as to why this ministry is so effective would be:

Prayer:

We always held special prayer gatherings before August to prepare for the month ahead and during the camp our prayer was intensified. Each morning the visiting preachers would lead a prayer gathering for all those who wished to attend. At the same time the staff would meet to eat their breakfast and then pray. These were outstanding times of praying and then seeing God move.

We would often highlight a group where we could see young people who were struggling or rebellious. It was extraordinary how many times in the evening gathering that day, they would respond to the Lord, and we would see remarkable changes in their lives. We would pray for an outpouring of the Holy Spirit and then know some of the most intense releases of the presence of God I have enjoyed in over 50 years of ministry.

Unity:

We also discovered the importance of the vital role that leaders and staff working together made towards the effectiveness of camp. We endeavoured to create a sense of vision and commitment towards a common goal which was to see lives changed by the power of God. The staff made a vital contribution, there was a sense in which those involved shared the burden and committed themselves to the goal of reaching these young lives for Jesus. This sense of commitment among the staff was instrumental in bringing a wonderful unity and common purpose where God works and moves freely.

I guess it is easier to create that for a week than it is in local church life over the whole year but for us it was a fundamental foundation that we worked hard to put in place and keep in place. The girls and guys in the kitchen sensing they were as involved as the preacher on the platform.

Ps 133:1,3. "Behold, how good and how pleasant it is for brothers to dwell together in unity! for there the Lord commands the blessing, life forevermore.

Word and Spirit:

Right from the beginning of the camp work we considered the preaching of the Word of God and the releasing of the Holy Spirit, to be the spiritual foundation that would result in changed lives.

We approached those who we considered the most effective communicators of Word and Spirit. We made a policy decision to make this a priority and to give ministry gifts that honoured those who made the commitment to be part of this work.

We attracted some of the best and most effective ministries in the movement we were part of. They were not necessarily the most well-known youth speakers, but we saw beyond that, believing that young people were able to hear and receive the Word of God without gimmicks or downgrading the message.

I can remember very powerful responses to the preaching, often resulting in many spending significant time in the Chapel following the evening meetings. Many being ministering to as they were impacted by the Word of God.

New and other expressions:

It is interesting to me that many other organisations and events have come into being in recent days, which recognise the power of being together in a spiritual atmosphere. Spring Harvest has touched many lives, New Wine has been an effective communicator of the Word and Spirit, Soul survivor developed into a major youth event touching thousands.

The various Bible Weeks of the "New Churches" around the country became "Holy Places" for many who encountered the presence and power of God. I believe God has made us to experience the phenomena of being together in this way. In the Old Testament the nation of Israel came together at least three times year and enjoyed an encounter with the living God.

I believe in the small and intimate, I believe in the development of a personal relationship with God, but I also believe that we need the wider, faith building, presence releasing dynamic, of the larger event to become all that God intends us to be.

Thought to ponder: *Are there other reasons this work is successful? Highlight the issues you feel are most significant.*

10

PROPHETIC ANOINTING AND IMPARTING THE HOLY SPIRIT

Acts 1:8. "But you shall receive power, the Holy Spirit coming upon you. And you shall be witnesses to Me."

1. Prophetic Anointing

Over the years God has used me from time to time as a channel for His prophetic word. My first awareness of carrying a prophetic anointing occurred in one of our first camps. I was sitting in the evening meeting at Chelsfield School in Kent in 1972 when during the worship I felt that Lord say to me, "I have given you a prophetic gift".

It came to me suddenly and unexpectedly and at that time I did not understand what it meant. Nevertheless, I knew the Lord had spoken to me. Later in that same meeting I felt the Lord remind me of the story in the Old Testament where David was instructed to move ahead when he *"heard the sound of rustling in the leaves of the trees" (1 Chron. 14:15)*. I felt the Lord say he wanted to move by His Spirit in this gathering and that young people would be filled with the Holy Spirit.

I brought this word to the meeting and the speaker for that gathering immediately responded and suggested that this was a moment for young people to be filled with the Holy Spirit. There were about 80 youngsters present and within 30 minutes around half of them had been filled with the Spirit, speaking in tongues, and experiencing the presence of God in a powerful way in their lives. This began a pursuing in my life of looking for and listening for the voice of God to be released in prophetic ministry.

Over the years I have continued to know times and seasons when I brought simple words of prophecy.

Corringham

It was in Corringham that we began to understand the importance of a broader dimension of ministry. Exploring the nature of the five-fold ministry gifts in Ephesians led to an understanding concerning the ministry of the prophet. I had begun to meet people who believed their primary ministry was as a "prophet" as Paul outlines in the book of Ephesians. *(Eph. 2:20,3:5,4:11)*. I began to seek God about this as it was suggested to me that this might be the area of gifting that God had released to me, alongside the teaching gift. I was challenged by this and set myself to seek God.

It was while I was convalescing following a hernia operation that I felt I received a clarity from the Lord concerning this matter.

As I spent time in the presence of God, I felt Him say to me that he had released to me a prophetic anointing, but it was not a permanent gifting or my main calling. Others seemed to be able to prophecy at will, I struggled with this, but I felt the Lord say to me that he would use me at times, that I would know an anointing that would come upon me at seasons and enable me in the prophetic. He said that at other times I would not experience that same awareness and I should not move unless inspired by the Spirit to proceed.

I found that very releasing and so from that time I have seen myself primarily as a teacher of the word of God who at times moves with and in a prophetic anointing. I recall some of the more prominent examples of being used by God in this way.

Nottingham

We were involved with the leaders of a church in Nottingham in organising a Bible Week in Peterborough. Mike and I had visited the church in Talbot Street to meet with the guys. They had a meeting that evening, and Mike had been invited to speak and so we stayed on for this gathering.

During the worship I felt God give me a very vivid picture. I saw the leaders of the church building a wall which had reached a certain height. I also saw in the background many others also building walls, but their walls were not as well built or as high. The Nottingham walls were more advanced than all the other walls. I felt the Lord say that there would be many churches who would look for help from Nottingham as they observed what God was doing and that they would become a source of apostolic help to many. I observed that they should keep building their wall as it was not finished but should also stand and support others in the building of their churches. I asked permission to share this word and was given the platform.

The leader of the church, who was quite an exuberant guy, called out loudly something like, "My God!". I knew the prophetic vision had touched something. He then stood up and said that during that morning the leadership had met to consider requests for help that were being received from other churches. They had then felt that God was calling them to move into this apostolic work. He felt this was a remarkable confirmation of what God was saying to them.

Zimbabwe

One of the most powerful prophetic experiences I had was in Zimbabwe. I had completed a week of training with leaders from around the nation and was due to speak on the Sunday morning at a large church in the centre of Harare.

During the Saturday evening, I could not sleep and found myself receiving a word from the Lord for the church in the nation for the next season. It was very clear and there was some very distinct language to describe what would be happening in the nation.

I had prepared a message but all through the worship that Sunday morning I felt this strong urge to bring this prophetic word. I stood to speak and said I felt the Lord had given me a prophetic word for them for the next season. Instead of preaching my prepared word I launched out into this word.

I spoke of "days of difficulty, of civil unrest and economic instability, of political intrigue and generally dark days. I then spoke of this being for the church "days of opportunity, that God would be with them, and they would enjoy days of growth and fruitfulness as they responded to the open doors which God would give them." I spoke of what would happen in the leadership of the nation and for the people. In fact, I prophesied for 25 minutes so never preached the word that I had prepared.

The extraordinary accuracy of this word as matters unfolded in Zimbabwe caused it to become a source of encouragement and strength to the church. The leader of the church where I preached felt it was so significant, he had it transcribed and sent it to many other leaders in the church around Zimbabwe.

Many churches who embraced the situation and understood what God was saying experienced significant growth. One leader we knew well who had a church on the outskirts of Bulawayo, saw his church grow from several hundred to thousands in a very short period.

The word was published and sent around many churches as a means of helping and supporting them during the very difficult circumstances the people of Zimbabwe were encountering.

Jamaica

Another prophetic moment occurred for me in Kingston, Jamaica. I was part of a team for a prophetic weekend and was invited to speak on the Sunday morning at the main church sponsoring the conference. This time it was during the meeting that I began to feel this prophetic stirring.

A word similar to the one I had brought to Zimbabwe was rising up within me. I could not tell you what songs were sung in the worship that morning or what contributions were made as I was wrestling with this word, which again was more than a simple prophetic encouragement and included some indications of what would be happening in the nation.

As I came to minister, I was trembling as I felt this awesome sense of responsibility for what I was about to say. The word was received in the usual way with many "amens" and vocal responses, but I also sensed it was a solemn moment. I spoke of some serious events that would take place in the country.

Again, when I had completed my prophetic mandate, I sat down. The leader of the church who also was involved with the political leaders of Jamaica insisted that we had heard from heaven. The outcome of that word was that it was released to the church in the country. Also, the audio recording was played in the national government and consideration was given to it by the Jamaican parliament.

Again, the contents were fulfilled in the days that followed. I saw the fulfilment of what I felt the Lord had revealed to me, but I only seemed to have that special prophetic anointing at times.

High Point

I also have experienced from time to time a prophetic word for churches. One of the most significant was released in High Point, North Carolina. Again, I felt I had this prophetic word, but I only received a couple of sentences.

As I had only received a few words I tried to dismiss the prompting of the Holy Spirit to speak them out. I stood to preach and opened my Bible. This is the only time in over 50 years that the following happened to me. I requested the congregation turn with me to the scriptures and tried to read. Three times I tried to read out the verses I had mentioned and three times I found that the words on the page did not make sense to me. I could not read them. Eventually, I gave in and prayed that the Holy Spirit would come and speak that morning.

I launched into the few prophetic phrases I had been given. As I spoke more came, then more. I would come to the end of a sentence and wait a few moments and it was as if I was receiving a download from heaven which I was to share. This happened over and over until after some 30 minutes I came to an end and knew that the word had been spoken.

There were words about worship, teaching, apostolic involvement, prayer and a number of other issues regarding the church. As I came to an end I stood still. I suggested that we wait quietly on the Lord for a moment having felt prompted by the Spirit to do so.

After a few seconds in that Holy quietness suddenly there was a massive thunderclap and rain began to pour down from the heavens. The church roof was metal, and the rain pounded on the roof with a sound like thunder.

This released an awesome sense of the presence of God. The Holy Spirit touched members of the congregation as we realised that this natural phenomenon was initiated by the Lord as a confirmation of His prophetic purpose.

Ruiru

Another time when I had prepared a message which was overtaken by a prophetic anointing was in Ruiru, a town just north of Nairobi in Kenya. I visited for the first time this pioneer church that had begun to grow and was some 50 people strong. It was led by a young man called Peter Chege who along with his wife Anne was establishing this church and school.

As I stood to speak, I was overcome with an awareness of the significance and strategic nature of this church and began to prophecy of growth and enlargement and influence. There were some specific characteristics that were highlighted in the prophecy.

Peter says it was a transforming word, confirming what he and Anne were holding in their hearts and creating faith to dare to believe that God would fulfil that word. Some 20 years later the church is now in a centre that seats some 2000 people, has many schools and a national ministry throughout Kenya serving in education and welfare matters including care for the poor and needy.

Peter is also the apostolic leader of a network of churches and provides teaching and training for leaders from the centre and in the region. He recently testified that every declaration made in that prophetic utterance has been fulfilled!

Belgium

Around the turn of this century, I visited Belgium twice a year over a period of time. One church that we regularly visited had enjoyed a period of blessing and growth until there were around 200 people meeting in a small town north of Brussels, the capital.

One Sunday morning as my message was coming to a conclusion, I felt the Holy Spirit drop a simple word into my heart. "There are people in this meeting who have engaged in sexual relationships outside of their marriage, if they do not repent and seek to put things right, I will expose their sin and it will be "shouted from the rooftops".

I felt the Lord was showing kindness and mercy to allow people to put things right. As I shared this, I was aware that it could be very embarrassing if I asked for a response. I asked the Lord for wisdom and felt I should encourage those to whom this word applied to sort things out during the day and come forward in the evening in response to a general response if they felt they needed prayer.

That evening the first couple out for prayer were leaders in the church. He had confessed to his wife he had been unfaithful some 14 years before and they had decided to work through this together and requested prayer. I asked the wife if she knew, and she replied she had known when it had happened but had no evidence so had carried it for all that time. Later, they became leaders in that church.

On the following Wednesday I received a telephone call from the leader of the church to let me know that during that week 14 couples had come for counsel and ministry up to that point.

On the Thursday I had a call from a young man who had recently married. Before his marriage he had had intercourse with several partners, he had been challenged to be faithful to his wife and asked if he could visit and receive prayer. He flew from Belgium to the UK the next day and we spent some time together.

This was a heavy word and required wisdom in its delivery. I believe the Lord helped me, but it was definitely not an enjoyable experience!

Camp

During our years leading the camp work I developed considerably in bringing words of encouragement of a prophetic nature to many. I would walk past individuals and receive clear words of direction.

I remember an instance with a young man from Scotland. There had been an appeal at the end of the ministry and as I walked past him, I felt the Lord say to me, He should be at the front responding to this challenge from the Word of God. I turned to him and suggested he respond, and he immediately ran to the front and was on his face before the Lord. He sought me out afterwards and said that he had been wrestling with the word that had been preached and as

I walked past said to the Lord, "If this word is for me and I should respond let Peter Butt confirm this".

I have many stories of that nature that occurred in those camp years. Over the years some have let me know what has happened to them in response to prophetic words I had brought them. I remember a young leader from Hanley called Kevin. Years later he told me how I had prophesied over him of the purpose of God for his life and how it was being fulfilled.

Peter Lyne

Probably the most remarkable personal word I brought was to a leader called Peter Lyne. He had been a major mover in the New Church movement in the UK. We were at a national Charismatic Leaders Conference. It took place at the beginning of the year. This particular year I went feeling tired and weary and not really feeling very spiritual at all. I think I had overindulged during the Christmas and New Year season and was feeling a little worse for wear.

We were encouraged to break into groups of four to pray for one another. I found myself in a group with Peter, I cannot remember who the other two in the group were. I did not know Peter well; in fact, we had hardly ever spoken to one another. As we stood together, I suddenly felt the Lord say to me that Peter was to move to New Zealand. So, I suggested this to him. He looked at me and said, "How do you know that, only my wife and I have discussed that possibility?" I suggested it might be revelation from the Lord.

We continued praying for one another and then I felt another prompting. I said to him. "You are 55 and this is the beginning of the most effective phase of your ministry. Like Smith Wigglesworth, who commenced his ministry later in life, God is going to use you like never before". I held my breath as I had no idea how old he was. He turned to me again and said how do you know I am 55. I again, suggested it might be the Lord had given me that information.

We set to pray again and once more I received further insight. I said to him. "You have a son named Simon; he is going to become Peter as he rises to stand alongside you in ministry." He turned to me and said that he had a son named Simon Peter. There were some tears and an awareness that this was a significant prophetic moment.

Lady in Czech Republic

I experienced a very powerful prophetic experience with a lady in the church at Hradec Kralove. My daughter and I were leading a prophetic teaching and training weekend and during the afternoon session I felt this strong urgency to bring a directional prophetic word. I said that there was a woman in the meeting who had decided that morning to emigrate to Australia. I suggested that the Lord was not in this, and that she should not go through with this decision. I offered to pray with this person.

During the break someone came up to me and said they were considering emigrating but had not yet made any decision. I prayed with this lady but knew it was not her. At the end of the evening service another woman came up to me and explained her situation.

She had experienced a very difficult year. She had lost her job, her long-term relationship with a guy had finished and that morning she had visited her parents instead of coming to the session and told them she was going to emigrate to Australia. She had been completely shocked by the accuracy of the word and knew that it was from God. I prayed with her and encouraged her to follow what the Lord was saying to her.

I visited the church again the next year and this lady came up to me, she said to me, "Do you recognise me". I must confess I did not! However, my mind was working overtime and I thought, maybe she is the Australian lady. I said, "Are you the lady I brought a word about not going to Australia". She replied that she was and then went on to tell me how that having made the decision to stay, she had acquired a brilliant job with more pay than she had ever received before, that she was in a new relationship that was going very well, and that she had found a new fulfilment in serving the Lord in the church, in a new role that had opened up for her. She was radiant!

This has not happened to me every day or every week but as promised from time to time this prophetic mantle has come upon me. I still *"earnestly seek the best gifts" 1 Cor. 12:31.*

Billy Kennedy

Billy had recently taken on the leadership of Southampton Community Church. The church had been through a difficult time, and it was my view that he needed to spend time building up the church and the people.

We held a leadership conference in Kampala, Uganda for all our East African connections and Billy was with me and others at that conference. While I was preaching one evening, I looked over at Billy who was seated on my right-hand side and as I did so felt a prophetic stirring and broke into my message to speak out the Word that I believed the Lord was giving me.

We had recently acquired the responsibility for overseeing two senior schools in our city and Billy had been instrumental in dealing with local government officials and government departments. I prophesied that what had happened was the beginning of God opening doors of influence and opportunity into the corridors of power. That Billy would find himself in situations where he would be able to influence those who were in authority, that he would meet with significant leaders within the nation. That God would use him because of his humility and openness to God. As I prophesied, I had a strange experience because what I was saying was not in line with my opinion about what Billy should give his time to.

Back in the UK this word began to be fulfilled in an amazing way with Billy being invited to be part of some national leaders' groups that opened doors of influence for him. He met dignitaries, Archbishops, leaders from the nation, attended a reception held by the then Prime Minister and was involved with national events where the queen and royal family were present. Whenever something happened that was part of the fulfilment of this prophecy Billy would text me and let me know where he was and who he was with. The Anglican church have even made him an honorary "Canon".

I have found that this experience of breaking into prophecy during preaching has been a common event with me over the years. I think when preaching you are perhaps more sensitive to God and able to be used more freely in this area.

Kings Lynn

I was preaching in Kings Lynn several years ago. The church was growing and their building was inadequate for the vision they carried. In the middle of preaching, I made a prophetic declaration it was along the lines that "God would provide a building that would result in them opening a well of healing in the centre of the town".

Several years later I was invited to be part of the ministry team to celebrate the opening of their new building in the centre of the town. They shared how they had acquired this property, a former theatre in a miraculous way. In the process of necessary renovation, a large lorry carrying building supplies turned up in the car park. The driver went into the building to report his arrival. Within a couple of minutes someone came scurrying into the building saying that the lorry was sinking into the ground. Mercifully they were able to move it before it disappeared into a large hole that appeared. Upon investigation, it was discovered that under the building was a large well which many years before had served the whole city of King Lynn with water.

This made such an impression on the church and encouraged their faith as it was a natural fulfilment of the prophecy I had brought. Upon further research they also discovered that the first hospital in Kings Lynn had also been on this site, so the "well of healing" was very significant in the prophetic purpose of God for the church.

Sheffield

I also felt, while preaching in Sheffield, that God was going to provide the church with a new place to meet as they had filled their current building. My actual words were, "God is going to give you a palace". They also received another word about the new building being half the price and twice the size. A large building that was a Bingo Hall became available.

When they sold their present building, they received twice as much money as the new hall cost, the new building also seated at least twice as many. When they began renovation work and stripped back the facia at the front of the building, they discovered it had previously been a dance hall.

Upon further excavation they restored the building to its original façade and discovered it has first been a cinema called, "The Palace". It is fascinating that it was several years after I prophesied that these words were fulfilled.

2. Imparting the Holy Spirit

My Experience

Another area of ministry where I seem to have been particularly used by God is in imparting the Holy Spirit. It is very clear in the book of Acts that after the initial outpouring of the Spirit and the special outpouring on those in the house of Cornelius that most people were filled with the Holy Spirit as hands were laid on them and the Holy Spirit imparted.

Acts 8:18. "And when Simon saw that the **Holy Spirit was given through laying on of the apostles' hands,** *he offered them money."*

From the moment I was filled with the Holy Spirit I recognised how important it was for every believer to receive the Holy Spirit. The encounter with the person of the Holy Spirit made such a difference in my life that I had a desire to see others filled with the Spirit.

AOG Conferences

Whenever there was an opportunity to pray for people to receive the Holy Spirit, I would offer myself as part of the team. The Assemblies of God conferences would hold a receiving meeting on at least one late night during the conference week. Between 200 – 400 people would be in those meetings. Usually, John Philips or Clyde Young, senior leaders in the movement, would inspire people to believe God for the promise of the Father and then a team of us would pray.

Those were exciting days of discovery and development for me as I learnt to inspire others with faith and encourage them to receive the Spirit. Without any pressure many would be filled with the Spirit and begin to speak in languages they had never learnt. As a young leader I aspired to be used by God in this way.

Dartford

I was invited to speak at a young people's area gathering on a Saturday evening. I was told there should be around 100 attending. As I prepared, I felt I should speak on the Baptism of the Holy Spirit and pray for people to receive Him. I also felt challenged to ask for 15 young people to be filled with the Spirit. At the end of the message 14 people came forward in response to the preaching. All 14 were filled with the Spirit. I was thrilled but also a little disappointed that I had not seen the 15th I had believed for.

At the end of the service as people were about to leave a young lady came up to me and said that she was too shy to come to the front but really wanted to be filled with the Spirit. I prayed for her and immediately all her shyness left as she spoke so loudly in other tongues that everyone still in the building turned round to see what the commotion was.

It was God filling this young lady with the Holy Spirit.

Guy in Clacton

There were also some interesting times of praying for individuals to be filled with the Spirit. Irene and I have always prayed about everything, including holidays. In about 1973, when we just had two small daughters, we were looking to take a holiday break.

I looked in a secular magazine and was intrigued by an advert offering a two-bedroom self-contained apartment in Clacton-on-Sea, Essex. There was nothing special about that, except that the advert went on to say, "Pentecostals Welcome". This so intrigued me that we booked a week in this place. The elderly couple that ran these apartments also lived on the premises.

During the week we had several conversations and I discovered that the elderly gentleman who had been a Christian for 16 years had been prayed with many times but had not yet been filled with the Holy Spirit.

On the Wednesday evening of our holiday, my wife went with the lady of the house to a mid-week service at their local church. I arranged to spend time with the guy whilst also babysitting. I encouraged him with the simplicity of receiving the Spirit, that faith was the key to entering into life in the Spirit. I then suggested we might pray together.

I began to prepare myself and speak quietly in tongues whilst moving towards the guy to pray for him. I was about 2 metres away from him when he began to shout out in languages given by the Spirit. It was just like the proverbial cork coming out of the bottle. He bellowed for a long period of time as the Holy Spirit exploded from within him. It truly was as Jesus said, *"He who believes on Me, as the Scripture has said, "Out of his innermost being shall flow rivers of living water." John 7:38.*

I have had the joy and privilege of praying for many individuals in this way and seeing them filled with the Holy Spirit.

Norman Young

I am sure our season in Walthamstow working with Norman Young was part of the purpose of God in developing this area of ministry. There were several brothers in the Pentecostal movement we were part of, whom God had used significantly in imparting the Holy Spirit. They were known as the "Young brothers".

I worked with one of them for several years and received encouragement from him in this area. People would visit our church from all over the region to have hands laid on them and receive the Spirit. It was again a privilege to be part of this work.

Camp

It was in the youth camp work that this ministry really developed for me. Each week I would ensure that at least one evening was given over to challenging the young people to be "filled with the Spirit". Most weeks at least 20 young people would receive the Holy Spirit, often it would be more and at times we saw up to 50 young people a week touched by the Holy Spirit.

Many of those young people had powerful encounters with the person of the Holy Spirit. I think I reached a place during those years when I believed that every person I prayed with would be filled with the Spirit; there was a measure of faith that I received from the Lord that gave me a boldness and confidence in this area which I have carried with me even up until today.

India

One highlight of recent years was in India with the Hindi speaking congregation of a church in Mumbai. I was at the end of a busy two-week ministry trip, and this was the last meeting on a Sunday evening. I was tired but the Pastor asked me to speak on the baptism of the Holy Spirit. I agreed but said I would not have the energy to pray for individuals but would pray over the whole congregation. There were around 120 people in the building. I preached through an interpreter and the first surprise came when I appealed for any who wanted to be filled with the Spirit.

The whole congregation stood to their feet expressing their desire to receive the Holy Spirit. As I prayed for the Spirit to fall upon them, around two thirds of the congregation were filled with the Spirit during a period of around 20 minutes. About 80 people immediately received the promise of the Father.

There was a group of young men on the front row; they all had a powerful encounter with the Spirit, with some staggering and some falling over as they spoke in tongues. Most of these young men are now in leadership within the church and are in teams involved in church planting.

The Pastor told me later he had sat next to a lady who arrived in the meeting and was a little drunk. She often called out and interrupted the meeting. The church had been trying to help her and she was responding to the gospel but struggling with an alcohol problem. He was astounded as he saw her filled with the Holy Spirit and speaking fluently in the language of the Spirit. As the Holy Spirit had come upon her, she had immediately become sober.

I am so grateful to God for the privilege I have experienced in seeing so many people Baptised in the Holy Spirit.

Thought to ponder: *Are you filled with the Holy Spirit?*

11

HOUSES AND CARS

As I mentioned earlier I have been part of the new church movement in the UK for a number of years. One of our major emphases has been the restoration of the five-fold ministries. At this point it would perhaps be helpful to take a fresh look at the apostolic and see how we far we have come on this journey.

It is important to acknowledge the tremendous vision and work of the initial leaders of this movement. They were pioneering a new kind of leadership; there were no models outside of the scriptures. There were no books to read and no one to turn to.

I appreciate the sacrifice they made. They faced opposition from many leaders of denominations and the established church in pressing through with this vision. My personal experience, as I made the transition from a Pentecostal denomination to the new churches, was that they imparted to us a love for God and the church. That is not to say they did not make mistakes or see the vision they carried fully implemented.

I believe we have a great opportunity to examine afresh the operation and functioning of the apostolic and this present re-emphasis on leadership is part of the journey originally initiated by the fathers of the new church movement. In the early days of the movement we sang great songs about "taking this land for Jesus", about "marching on this land", about "this being the time". The truth is that the restoration of apostles and prophets in the way we implemented it has not produced what we envisioned!

Thank God for all that has happened, but I believe the model has weaknesses that require attention. What we have built has not produced the goods. A great friend of mine who has been part of this movement made this simple observation:

"Instead of the apostolic serving the churches the churches have ended up serving the apostolic. Everything comes back in to the centre, instead of out from the centre".

I look at some of our expressions of team and see that we have not pressed on into new wineskins but reverted to the old. I observe many new churches expressing more of a pastoral than a missional model and even using the "pastor" title again!

One of my observations is that we did not give enough attention to a variety of giftings and encourage different people with different personalities to work together. Our teams become people of like-minded gifts with like-minded personalities, doing like-minded activity. Instead of the freshness of complementary giftings we merely produced rotas of different people with the same gifting, taking the meetings but doing the same thing.

At one time, I was sharing with a guy who had given up a high-powered government job in the Civil Service to serve in a ministry team. After some time striving to maintain his integrity and struggling to find his place, he found it necessary to find another place to work out his call. His comment was that, because he did not like curry or laugh out loud at the humour shared by the team, he found himself marginalized.

I was speaking recently with a professor at our local university who has been part of the new church scene since it came into being. Our conversation turned to this book I am writing; both he and his wife asked if I had seen an apostolic team functioning as we envisioned. I replied I had seen glimpses of what I believed was an apostolic model, but not a full-orbed expression. His comment about our history, was that there were too many "egos" that got in the way and had not allowed the vision to flourish. An interesting viewpoint.

I would like to look afresh at some biblical expressions of the apostolic that perhaps are not too prevalent in today's teams. Perhaps we can learn from what we have experienced and be part of the new wineskins that are required for this new day.

Mindsets

One of developments of these past few decades has seen a changing understanding of the importance of mindsets. It has become popular to talk about paradigm shifts or changes. Most of my generation and certainly the generation of the older apostolic leaders were educated by a system that came about as a result of the enlightenment, in a rational and scientific way. Everything had to be evaluated and conclusions had to be reached which satisfied the mind and reason. In more recent times this has come to be known as the "modern mindset".

There is nothing wrong with that except that it limits our approach to spiritual things and can affect our application of biblical truths. We are inclined to approach things in a structural way rather than an organic way. We are more about organization and order than developing organic relationships.

I remember when we sought to introduce house groups to build relationships. We had the revelation of meeting in homes rather than mid-week meetings in the church building. A book was written about these small groups called "Wednesday night at 8". We had seen the truth and importance of building relationships but our mindset saw it in terms of organizing a meeting rather than organic life.

This is not a criticism of the book, but an observation of how we had been educated to think and apply truth. Perhaps the chart below will help to show the different emphases

Contrast of Organic and Structured.

Organic.	**Organisational.**
Flexible.	Rigid Structures
Constantly changing.	Static
Allows for new growth.	Hampers growth.
Grows organically	Requires constant supervision
Requires tending.	Requires maintenance.

I suggest we had a revelation but the way we applied what we saw was flawed.

There is nothing new about these different mindsets. They were in operation in Paul's day and he understood them. He saw the difference between the Jewish and Greek process of thinking and evaluating issues. Paul said, *"For the Jews ask for a sign, and the Greeks seek after wisdom;"(1Cor 1:22).*

There was a different framework or mindset between the Jewish and Greek way of processing information. The following table might illustrate this and help us to understand this matter.

Understanding mindsets.

Hebrew	**Greek**
Celtic	Roman
Catholic	Reformed
Evangelical	Charismatic
Denominational	New church streams
Modern	Post –modern

Many years ago, I read the classic book of the history of the church in this country. "The Ecclesiastical History of the English People" by Bede. It provides fascinating insight into the struggle between the Celtic and Roman mindsets in the church, the Roman wanting to organize and structure everything and the Celtic wanting to depend on the Holy Spirit to lead and to guide.

Eventually the Roman influence took ascendancy and the activity of the Holy Spirit was replaced with form and order which laid the foundation for what history calls "the dark ages."

This was the period of spiritual barrenness which existed until the reformation. I believe we have an opportunity to change the influence of that mindset in this generation and see a fresh apostolic movement break out among us.

I have often heard leaders of large churches describe the way they organize their communities. Some of the words they use to describe their operations really concern me. They use the imagery of a well-run factory to describe the running of their church and its gatherings. They say things like, "Our church runs like a well-oiled machine!"

I am certainly not appealing for chaos and disorder, I believe we should be striving for excellence in everything we do. However, I do find it difficult to relate the biblical revelation of the church to a factory. God is revealed as a gardener not a CEO!

In the Bible, most of the parables of Jesus were based on organic pictures. He spoke about seeds and growth and trees and only rarely used static pictures to describe the Kingdom of God. It is interesting that when Peter talks about the church as a building, he uses the description of *"living stones" (1Pet.2:5)*. In every one of Paul's letters he uses the organic picture of "a body" to describe the church. He illustrates the functioning of the church by using this direct parallel, calling the church *"the body of Christ". (1Cor.12:12-27)*.

When Jesus speaks of the Father, He never speaks in terms of Managing Director or Chief Executor Officer. He does not use military terminology either. He speaks of God as a Gardener.

"I am the real vine, and my Father is the gardener. (John 15:1)

The model is a gardener not a CEO/Manager. The vision of the gardener Is to prepare the ground and provide the environment for things to grow. It is not the image of running a factory (like a well-oiled machine). It is about providing enough structure for the plants to grow on their own, to their full potential.

The structure is minimal, too much structure hampers and crushes the growth. The plants require pruning but the purpose of any restriction is for more growth! The challenge of the gardener is to prepare the ground for growth, to create an environment for the plant to flourish.

I have a picture in my mind of leaders seeing themselves as managers in the factory and looking over the shoulder of the workers ensuring they are doing the job correctly. I do believe that in some cases the structure of the church imitates this model. I believe it is not the best model and we would do well to consider what is perhaps, a more biblical picture.

We also find God is revealed as a Shepherd. *(Is.40:11, John 10.11,14)*. In the previous chapter on the shepherd we pointed out that the shepherd leads the sheep, he doesn't drive them. We really are not butchers but shepherds. Jesus was very clear; 16 times in the Gospels he said, *"Follow me" (John 10:27)*.

With that foundation in mind, let us look with fresh eyes at the scriptures…

12

FRESH APPROACHES TO THE APOSTOLIC

Matt 6:33 "But seek first the kingdom of God and His righteousness; and all these things shall be added to you".

David Matthews prophecy

The first time I came across David Matthews he spoke at a Team Spirit leaders' event in Pilgrims Hall, Brentwood. Little did I know then I would work with him for several years. He did not know me beyond my name, and that I was part of the leadership team at Thurrock Christian Fellowship. He preached on *2Cor.10:12-15*.

I was impressed with his message about living within the boundaries of the gifting God has given us. At the end of his sharing, he addressed me directly and simply said, "God will add to you houses, cars and finance". It was not something I was expecting or looking for but nevertheless it has been our experience that we have seen the provision of God in our lives in all those areas.

Hornchurch – Baptist Manse

As I mentioned in the chapter where God called us to leave Walthamstow. We were left with nowhere to go as we lived in a house owned by the church. We were a young family with four young children. My mother suggested we could stay with her for a short time, so we responded to her goodwill and the six of us slept in one room. My mother knew many people in our hometown of Hornchurch and told those she connected with what we were doing.

We had only been in her house for two days when I received a called from the secretary of the local Baptist church. The conversation went something like this, "Our minister has just left and our new minister in not coming for another six months. We heard you were in the area and wondered whether you would help us out by living in our church manse. We would not charge you any rent and would just ask you to pay the house bills."

This large detached four bedroomed house with a study was in one of the most sought-after residential areas in the town. God had gone before us to provide us with a place to live. It is probably the most exclusive property we have lived in.

Corringham

The six months were coming to an end, and nothing was working out for our next accommodation. We had been given a significant amount of money to put into the project we felt the Lord was leading us into. The youth camp work was growing, and we were certain we had moved correctly in response to the prophetic leading we had received. We had produced our youth camp brochure for that year, and it was being printed by a church in Corringham who had a printing press at that time. The children were at school, so Irene came with me to travel the 15 miles to collect the printed brochures.

On the journey we spoke together about our situation, that we needed to find a place for our family to live. We spoke of money we had been given towards the project, and decided that it would be right to use it in the interim period to purchase a house for us to live in. We arrived at our destination and as we drew into the car park both agreed that we should buy a house with the money we had in hand.

We entered the church building and saw the leader, Mike Godward at the front of the building. We called out our greeting and he responded and then said, "Do you know anybody who wants to buy a house?" It was so remarkable that we replied, "Yes us.....we'll have it" before we had even seen it or knew the price. Of course, we discovered the house was perfect, the right price and located brilliantly for us and the family. That led to 9 years of fruitful family life, exciting church life and the development and growth of both my ministry and that of Irene. I see the providence of God clearly in that situation.

We had no desire, knowledge or leading towards Corringham but God arranged another Divine appointment to lead us into His purpose for our lives.

We did not have a distinct prophetic word on this occasion but knew the hand of God on our lives.

Brentwood

When it came to the end of our season in Corringham and we felt the Lord leading us to connect with Team Spirit and particularly John Noble. We looked to move to Brentwood to be near where I would be working.

We put our house on the market with a view to buying a property in Brentwood. It was the season of very high interest and resulted in a major property collapse that saw many people's houses repossessed and many others experiencing what became called, "negative equity", where they owed more money on the property than it was worth.

We prayed and looked to God. Nobody came to view our property and we spent many hours looking at houses in the Brentwood area, but nothing was available that suited our purposes or was within our price range. All the advice we received from experts and friends was to invest in property. However, we kept praying and nothing seemed to work out either in buying or selling.

Eventually, we felt the Lord led us to a large property to rent in an ideal location and so proceeded with this venture. The house we owned in Corringham did not have any people viewing it let alone offering to buy it. The weekend we secured the house to rent we decided to put the house in

Corringham up for rent and use the money received to pay the rent on our new abode.

I telephoned the estate agent on the Monday following the weekend we had decided this course of action. The guy answered the phone and said, "I was just about to ring you, we have a couple in the office who have been let down in a property sale and your property looks ideal for them, can I send them round."

I explained our decision and said I had called to take the property of the market. He appealed to me to allow them to visit with the suggestion that if they did make an offer, we could always refuse it as they were unlikely to consider paying the full price for the house. I agreed and a young man and his wife came to view the house.

I was in the frame of mind to deter them from buying the property and purposely made them aware of the all the faults in the house. I said, the garden is very small to which the guy responded, "That is good I hate gardening." I showed them the house extension and said it had taken up so much of the garden and was not built to a very high specification and he replied, "That is fine, I am a model train enthusiast, and it will be ideal for my hobby".

As we walked around the house, every obstacle I suggested was met with a positive response until I was laughing inside. I felt like the Lord had arranged this at exactly the correct time. By the time we had completed the viewing I knew they were going to make an offer. I tried to put them off, but they looked at one another and said to me, "We would like to buy this house from you, and we will pay the full price". I felt like this appointment had been engineered by the Lord and so accepted their offer and the sale went ahead.

Basildon

This left us in a difficult position. We had a certain amount of cash and wondered how we should invest it. After prayer we decided to buy a property in a nearby town called Basildon. The property prices were less than the immediate area and after paying our small mortgage we had enough built money to purchase a house for £53,000.

We found a property for that amount and found a Christian couple to rent it from us. It worked extremely well for several years. I include these details, and that it was what was known as a "concrete house" rather than the usual brick house that we have in the UK, for a reason.

Following several years of renting during which we saved around £10,000 in very high mortgage fees as the interest rate in the UK soared to over 10% and even in some cases 15%, we began to look at buying a property in Brentwood. Properties prices had reduced and come down from their extortionate value and were now reasonably priced.

We put the Basildon property on the market and discovered that it had reduced in value by nearly £10,000. This shocked us and was a problem for us, we could not sell the house and the best offer we received was £39,000, more than £14,000 less than we paid for it.

We seriously prayed and sought the Lord. Irene and I were abroad on a missions trip when our daughter advised us when we telephoned home that the local government were going to compulsorily purchase our house due to an outbreak of "concrete cancer". We had never heard of such a thing.

Apparently, these concrete houses can develop a problem where they crumble and disintegrate if they have not been treated correctly. We arrived home a little distressed and uncertain what this would mean. We knew what the value of the house was and wondered what offer we might receive. We heard that because this property had been previously government owned and was one in a block of four attached houses, a central government office would make us an offer. We waited and eventually the offer came.

We opened the envelope with some trepidation to find that they had offered us £55,000, more than we had paid for the building although properties had dropped considerably in price. We were overjoyed as this meant we had more potential to buy a house. We accepted the offer to be told two weeks later that they had agreed to add another £1500.

We could not believe the goodness of the Lord. As I mention in the provision of finance chapter, we also received another sum of money later.

Brentwood – Warescot Road

We were then able to purchase a house in central Brentwood. We discovered a house that had been re-possessed which was offered at a good price. We worked out our costs and offered appropriately. Our offer was turned down as too low.
We waited prayed again and the put in the same offer which was accepted. We were able to restore the house to an

excellent condition and lived happily for several years before moving to Southampton. When we came to put the house on the market, we discovered we had made an excellent investment with the property now worth far more than we had paid for it. By following the Lord through those years, we probably saved between £25,000 and £30,000.

We invited an estate agent to view the house on around 8th December, it was a Friday. The agent advised us of its value, and we agreed to put it on the market for the top value. He then suggested that we leave it until the new year to put it up for sale and he had been in the business for 17 years and had never sold a house that near to Christmas. He said it would take a miracle.

When he said those words, I felt a rising in my spirit. I said to him, "We are Christians and believe in miracles. We believe that God answers prayer and would like you to put the house on the market immediately". He replied that he would arrange for it to go on sale on the next Monday.

I was away but that Monday afternoon Irene received a call from the agent to say there was a couple interested in viewing the house. They came round, viewed the house, and put in an offer for the full value of the property. The estate agent rang me, and his first words were, "You have got your miracle".

The house was sold.

Southampton – Portswood

Finding a house to live in in Southampton was a difficult experience. We had an area we would have preferred to live in. We needed a large house as one of my daughters, her husband their one child along with our son were intending to live with us.

We visited the area on several occasions and although we visited a large number of properties nothing came alive for us. One day we had spent the whole day looking at houses and had again been frustrated. I suggested before we drive back to Essex some 2 hours away, we pay a final visit to an Estate Agent we had not yet visited.

They provided us with several details of houses in the area and we began the drive home. Irene, my wife was looking at the properties and she came across one and said that it looked like it had everything we needed. I suggested we look at it next time we came down to the area, but she felt stirred by this house and requested we at least take a look at it.

We visited this house and sat outside. My wife then suggested I knock on the door and ask if we might view the house. I thought this was an outrageous request. In the UK visits are arranged by Estate Agents and it would be considered out of order to violate that code. The owners of the house, who would not have a clue who we were would be perfectly in their rights to refuse our request.

After protest I approached the house and was surprised when the owner allowed us to view the property. Irene immediately believed this was the house for us and within a few minutes I too was overwhelmed by its suitability for us and our family.

It was only on the journey home after my wife had expressed her pleasure at the property that I made her aware that it was not in the area we had been looking. Somehow that did not matter anymore but in other circumstances we probably would not have looked at it. The price was excellent and within weeks we found ourselves in this house.

Bitterne – Tom Tyers

After a couple of years, the family moved into their own place and the house became too large. We prayed and felt we should move. We looked for a property and settled on one that seemed right for us. However, after about 6 months the owners decided not to sell. We had already sold our house so were in a difficult position.

We seriously prayed and found an unusual house on 3 floors that overlooked the river and the city centre. We made an offer that was accepted and began the procedure to purchase. Suddenly, without warning the buyer backed out as the property they were looking at had fallen through. In this period coming up to Christmas we visited a church we were helping in Essex and enjoyed a meal with them.

At the end of the evening one of the guys called Tom who knew nothing of our plans and situation came over to us and said, "Are you buying a house? Only I saw an unusual house on 3 floors overlooking a river and felt to encourage you to say that the Lord has it all in hand, it is yours".

Imagine our response! Two days later the agent came back to us with the news that everything was now on course for the sale if we were still interested. We lived in that house for 18 years.

Eastleigh

Again, the time came for us to downsize as we found ourselves on our own. We prayed and were invited to move to Eastleigh by the leaders of the church who happened to be our son-in-law and daughter.

Finding a house was again an interesting exercise of seeking to hear from the Lord about where we were to live. A couple of houses did not work out until we found our present property which has proved to be ideal. Again, the leading of the Lord was part of our decision-making process.

Church buildings

Another area where we have seen the Lord work for us in is, church buildings. In all the places we have lived we have also been involved in seeing property acquired or extended for the Kingdom of God.

Barnet

I have already mentioned in several places the story of us totally replacing the building in Barnet. It was an amazing exercise in faith for a young leader and a small group of committed people. It was said of the people around Nehemiah that they had *"a mind to work." Neh.4:6.*

Every week a small group of people would gather to work and rebuild the church. Some friends from other churches with skills that were required, gladly gave their time and even their money to support this work. In 6 months, the property was transformed and opened completely debt free.

I read an article about that time carrying advice about building churches. I discovered that we had hardly done anything according to the book! That was not because we were arrogant, but because we just did what we felt the Lord was showing us and we saw the project completed.

Walthamstow

During our time in Walthamstow, we again saw the building developed to increase the capacity, after we moved on it was developed again to house the growing congregation.

Brentwood

While in Brentwood we saw a quite remarkable provision of a property. We were a growing church, the small chapel that belonged to the church was too small and quite inadequate, so we were meeting in hired buildings, usually schools.

At that time, I was in a season of prayer and fasting and would often walk as I prayed. On one such occasion I walked along a path behind my house and found myself in a quiet country lane. I walked towards the main road to find my way. I passed a building on the left. It was hidden behind some trees but had a driveway and a wide gate leading to a car park area.

I had never seen this building before. I walked on past and then felt prompted to go back and take a look. I walked into the property to find an empty building on a considerable plot of land. It had a large hall and several other rooms and facilities.

I looked through the window to discover that it was a training centre for "Martins", a well-known retailer at that time. It did not look as though it was being used. Next door on another large plot was a mansion which had been converted into offices and was the headquarters of this company.

I wrote down the telephone number and when I arrived home, I telephoned the company and was put through to their buildings director.

It was rather an unusual conversation. I mentioned the building and asked if it was for sale, to be told they were not sure what to do with the property. I asked if they would consider that, and he agreed to make a request to the directors of the company. He came back with the suggestion that we make an offer. We took professional advice to be told that it was worth at least £500,000.

We met as a leadership team to consider the way ahead. Various suggestions were made but I felt we should go away and pray and come back with a figure that we felt the Lord gave us. One week later we met again. There were various figures presented most around £200,000/300,000. I had felt the Lord say to me we should offer £65,000.

When I first made my suggestion there was a quite negative response. Almost a feeling that they would not consider us to be serious in offering such a derisory figure. I continued to state my case, really believing the Lord had given it to me.

Eventually there was an agreement that we should press ahead. We agreed to make an offer of £60,000 giving us the ability to raise it another £5000 should that be necessary. I think there was a feeling that the offer would be rejected out of sight.

It was a week later that the building director of Martins came back to us. He said they had considered our offer and were not willing to take £60,000 but would accept £65,000. He then went on to explain that at the directors meeting most of those present had felt this was a poor offer and that the building was worth far more. However, the new managing director, who had just been appointed said, "As you know I am a Christian believer and if we accept this offer, I believe God will bless our business and that we will not suffer financially". The directors responded to his challenge, and we were able to buy this property for £65,000 when it was worth probably, £500,000.

Throughout my years of ministry, I have heard and seen marvellous stories of God's provision for His people in the miraculous supply of buildings and finance to build His church both literally and spiritually.

Cars

As the prophetic word I received from David Matthews mentioned cars I thought I would include a paragraph on this matter. We have always prayed about changing our car and such things. I could write a whole chapter on the matter.

However, I just want to comment that every time we have felt it was time to change our vehicle, we have experienced something of God's leading in the process. Sometimes we have been offered vehicles at extraordinarily good prices, other times we have just been aware that God was in the transaction. We can truly say that God has blessed us in this area.

Thought to ponder: *Call to mind your own stories of Gods' provision and give Him thanks!*

13

PROVISION: DAILY BREAD

Phil 4:19 "But my God shall supply all your need according to His riches in glory by Christ Jesus."

Irene and I have experienced the provision of God throughout our ministry. In over 50 years of serving God, we have only received a full salary for around five of those years. The rest of the time God has provided for us through various means. Sometimes supernatural provision, sometimes providing a means of earning money alongside our ministry, sometimes through churches and friends who felt moved to support us.

Our testimony is that we have never been overdrawn, never had a bill we could not pay and never been hampered from doing what we felt the Lord had called us to. Several years ago, a friend mentioned to me that he would love to do what I was doing, teaching, and travelling around the world. He then commented, "But I could never afford it". My response was, "Then you will never do it because I have never been able to afford it either, but I know God has called us to this work and am confident He will provide". I have always felt I will know it is time to stop travelling when the provision stops.

Near the beginning of our journey after we moved on from Walthamstow, we enjoyed the company of a couple of friends for a weekend. The lady was into tapestry and embroidery and had prepared a bible verse in a picture frame for us to enjoy. It read:

"But… My God shall supply all your need according to His riches in glory by Christ Jesus". Phil. 4:19

The interesting thing is that the word *"But"* was embroidered in a line on its own followed by several full stops. As I looked at the frame, I felt it was a personal message directly to me.

Not many of us have first names that appear in the scriptures even fewer of us have both our first and surname in the Bible! It has become a means of encouragement to believe God for us over the years.

Bible College

Coming from a middle-class suburb of Essex I had everything provided for me as a child. When the call of God came, I had to provide the fees for my two years at Bible College. It was a fresh challenge. In those days very few students were able to acquire grants and we had to provide our own finance.

I managed the first year reasonably well but ran out of finances in the middle of the first term of my second year. I visited the principal of the college and expressed my predicament, feeling that if God had called me, He would provide.

The counsel I received was that I should wait for a month and see what happens. During that month I received news that the fees for the remainder of that term had been paid. This was my first experience of God's provision of finance. I have no idea to this day who paid those fees as I did not let anybody know of my situation.

There were then just two terms left to the end of the course. I worked during the winter break and earned enough from part-time work for the first few weeks of the term. As I came towards the time when my fees would be due, I began to seek the Lord. I had made plans, believing them to be in the will and purpose of God.

Irene and I had planned to marry in the August at the end of the course, I had felt God was leading us to take on leadership of a church, that God had called me to ministry. I came before God and prayed something like this. "God, you know my heart, you know the things I am considering, I want to be obedient to your will for my life. If these decisions I am about to make are in line with your purpose for our lives please confirm it by providing the remainder of the fees for my Bible College Course".

Every morning the post was placed in a rack on the wall by the main entrance of the college. There was a letter for me the morning after I had prayed. I opened the letter to discover that the sender was requesting to know the sum of the fees I had yet to pay as the Lord had moved upon his heart to supply these funds.

The extraordinary thing about this is that the letter was posted before I had prayed. I had this sense of affirmation and confidence that as God had called me, He could provide for us. This was the beginning of a journey of faith when it comes to finance.

Barnet

I have already indicated the provision of God for a part-time employment role when we were in Barnet. God was very good to us, and our church finances increased during our five years in north London. We also were able to complete an extensive building programme. The building still had an outstanding mortgage on it when we arrived and the tired, old place needed a complete renovation.

We prayed and received a remarkable gift of £5000, which in 1971 would have enabled us to buy several houses. The cost of clearing the mortgage and updating and upgrading the building was £10,000, and we were able to open the new place debt free.

We saw the provision and supply of heaven during this venture with stories too numerous to tell. Electricians, plumbers, builders giving their time and energy as well as an army of volunteers from the church itself.

I tell one story of provision that was very real to me personally. We required six new doors for the building, each one the same size. I explored the prices of new doors and found that they were very expensive. At that stage we were short of the necessary funds coming near the end of the building programme.

I was driving through a town near to our home when I spotted a hardware store. I felt a constraint to stop and go in. In fact, I had driven past and had to drive back to the store, such was the impetus of the Holy Spirit. I walked in and looked at the doors they were selling and found they were all far too expensive for our budget.

A shopkeeper came over to help me and asked what I needed. I told him six new doors all the same size for our new church building but that the doors on show were too expensive. He requested that I follow him. We went through the store to the warehouse and by the rear entrance were 6 doors. They were all brand new but with the hinges already cut out. They were also stained with a mahogany finish. They happened to be the size we required. He explained to me that a customer had acquired the doors but had cut the hinges in the wrong place and so had to purchase six more doors. He had left the doors behind for the store to dispose of. The owner of the shop said that if I gave him £1 for each door, he would be happy for me to take them off his hands. We were blessed and delighted…

It was yet another affirmation of the hand of the Lord upon the project. Again, it was a faith builder for this group of believers to see God provision.

We had a very lovely experience of God's provision for our personal needs during this time. Irene was expecting our second child and did not have an outdoor coat that was able to cover her growing body as we were approaching the coldest part of winter.

We prayed and the next day we received a cheque in the post from the Inland Revenue for £20. I have no idea to this day why we received this money as I had not applied for a tax rebate. Irene visited the shopping centre to see there was a maternity coat reduced from £70 to £20 in a shop window. It fitted exactly and she was able to purchase it immediately.

It was an extraordinary example of the goodness of God.

Walthamstow

On the week before we moved out from Walthamstow my wife and I discussed how much money we would require to give my mother to take care of our family for each week we were with her. We came up with a figure that we thought was reasonable.

On the day we moved house, just as we were finalising clearing out the house, a lady called Ivy from the church called round. Irene had already left, and I was about to drive away. She said, "I am glad I caught you I wanted to give you your Christmas card". I thanked her, put the card in my jacket pocket and thought to myself that this was a little unnecessary and forgot about it.

Later when settled in my mother's house, and having stored our furniture, I was in the kitchen with my wife and my mother when I remembered Ivy giving me the card. I took it from my jacket pocket and opened the card. As I did so several £5 notes floated to the ground. I picked them up… quickly… and proceeded to count them. It was the exact amount Irene and I had discussed we would need to cover our living expenses. Another indication of the care and provision of God.

Some months later I mentioned this to Ivy when we saw her at a church gathering, and she told me that the Lord clearly spoke to her that morning and told her to give us that exact amount of money. A wonderful beginning on our journey of faith.

Kings Lynn

We have many stories of God's provision in many ways, but some stand out. We were invited to speak at the church of our friend, Paul Randerson in Kings Lynn. We had recently returned from Nigeria where we had witnessed some outstanding miracles which had inspired us.

As I shared some of the wonderful accounts of supernatural activity, I suddenly looked at Paul and prophesied to him, "You must visit Nigeria". I then continued preaching.

After a couple of minutes, I felt another urge of the Spirit and said to him, "And I will pay your fare". As soon as I said it, I thought where am I going to get the £500 to cover this? I looked at my wife and a look of horror had appeared on her face. I knew what she was thinking!

We enjoyed lunch together, and then on our way back to our home in Southampton we stopped at a church in

Brandon to preach in their evening service. We had a good time and as I went to leave the building a gentleman who I did not know, placed a folded piece of paper in my shirt pocket and said, "This is for you." When I arrived at my vehicle, I took the folded paper and opened it to discover it was a cheque for £500.

Within 5 hours of me making that statement of faith God had provided the means!

Electric Bill

There are days when my faith is not all it should be, God has never failed us or let us down but on a few occasions, I have wavered and wondered how I would complete some payments. On one such occasion I received a substantial electric bill and did not have the funds to cover it in our accounts. I talked to the Lord about it and tried to get to sleep that night. I had a restless night worrying about this payment even though we have seen God work for us so many times.

The next morning in our mail there was a letter addressed to me from Ongar in Essex. I did not recognise the handwriting on the envelope and opened it with interest. There was a note which stated that this man we knew, called Gavin had felt moved by the Lord to send us a cheque and so enclosed was this cheque for the amount of the bill. I have never received a gift from this guy before or since that time.

The startling thing about this is that the letter was sent before I called on the Lord and spent the night wondering and worrying where the money would come from. This was the second time I had experienced the reality of the statement in Isaiah.

And it shall come to pass, that before they call, I will answer; and while they are yet speaking, I will hear. Isaiah 65:24

The money was already on the way before I had begun to get anxious! Another lesson on trusting the Lord!

Fares

I have already mentioned that the God who called us to teach and train leaders in the developing world has always provided the means for us to travel. In recent years we have some great supporters who have contributed towards this.

In the early days of travel, it was not like this. We had made a commitment to visit South Africa and had purchased our tickets. The day was fast approaching when the charge for the fares would need to be met and the bill paid. I mentioned in the chapter on houses the way God had not only led us but provided for us in a most unusual way through the house we had purchased in Basildon.

Everything had been settled for the sale and the monies had been received by us. Then a couple of months later and the day before I had to pay for the flights to South Africa, we received another letter from the council purchasing the house. They said this was the last payment they would make but they had become aware that the moving from their houses had been disruptive to many families, so were making a payment of £750 to each house owner. You have probably already realised that this was the amount of my fare to South Africa.

God's provision and timing was perfect.

Heart Operation

In 2002 I underwent open-heart surgery and had a triple by-pass operation. It was another experience where I found the Lord so faithful. It also meant I was unable to teach and train and fulfil my ministry, and so as a self-employed man I had no income.

The wonderful provision of God was so powerful over those 12 weeks of inactivity that my bank balance was higher at the end of the period than before. We received gifts from friends and churches from around the country. One couple sent a personal gift of £1000. This was the only time we received from them in this way. God has never let us down.

I also believe that the 12 weeks convalescence that was enforced on me was a life-changing experience that has resulted in the development of the work of School of Ministries. I had returned from India and run out of the medication I used for high-blood pressure. Several days later I had visited the local shopping centre when I felt this extraordinary pain in my chest. It was as if an iron band had been put around my chest and someone was tightening it. I thought I was going to pass out and die.

My first thought was to talk to the Lord. I said something like, "Well Lord I thought I had longer and more work to do but if this is the end, I am ready". I have heard stories of people's lives flashing before them and all sorts of other experiences but for me it was quite analytical and despite the pain, I was thinking quite clearly. I stood still, unable to move, expecting at any moment to collapse in a heap. However, after about 20 minutes the pain subsided, and I continued with my business.

I visited the hospital for tests and Irene and I were invited to meet with the consultant. He suggested I required a triple by-pass as my arteries were in poor shape. I responded by asking if I could complete several ministry engagements in Belgium and India that were planned. He put his pen down on the table, looked me in the face and said, "Mr Butt if you visit India, they will bring you back in a box". I think that brought home to me how serious my condition was.

I came to a place of peace about the whole matter and believed that God was preparing an opportunity for me to have an enforced sabbatical. It seems most leaders in churches are granted one every 7 years or so. I had been going for over 30 years without any such break. I began to look forward to it, declaring that even if the Lord healed me, I would take this time from active ministry.

The operation and time in hospital went extremely well. The evening before the event the nurse arrived with a cup of water and some sleeping pills. She suggested I would need them. I said that as a Christian I believed that God would give me the sleep I needed. She said that she would still leave them on the bed-side cabinet in case I required them.

She expressed her surprise when she returned in the morning to find them still on the cabinet and said, "Oh you really did not need them then". It was an opportunity to share the gospel. I also awoke that morning of the operation with a song on my heart and mind, I think I may have been singing it quietly. It was that old hymn:

"Leaning, leaning, leaning on the everlasting arms, leaning on Jesus, leaning on Jesus, leaning on the everlasting arms"

Irene had a group of ladies praying for me during the operation and it went remarkably well. I was up and about within 36 hours, home within 5 days and walking freely for an hour a day within 2 weeks. I then enjoyed 10 weeks of reading, refreshment, revelation, and sunshine. It was summer and I was able to relax in our garden. God spoke to me clearly though that time from John's gospel and the many other books I read.

SOM Provision

Although we have let people know about our projects in our teaching and training work and although on occasions we have produced literature, our main thrust for raising funds has been prayer. I know this might sound very kind of spiritual but nevertheless it is true.

Apart from one school we planned we have always seen the supply of heaven on this work. The school that the money did not come in for proved to be a place where we should not get involved and so we were saved from a difficult situation.

Graham

At one time we required £2000 for a school which we did not have money available for. We felt we should pray and if the money did not come by the end of the month, which was two weeks away, we should cancel the school.

Graham Bower who at that time was leading a church had received a word of knowledge one Sunday morning that someone in the church was seriously struggling financially and that God was going to do a miracle for her and her family. He offered to pray for anyone that was in that situation.

A lady came forward and explained that her husband had cancer and was unable to work, that they were 6 months behind with their mortgage payments and in debt with the bank. It was a serious position. That week she received an unbelievable amount of money from her uncle who had come into a large amount of money. She paid all her debts, had money to spare and in gratitude to God gave School of Ministries a gift of £2000!

Not all our provision has come in such a dramatic way, but we have seen God work for us in wonderful ways that have enabled us to teach and train leaders all over the world.

Ladies praying

Over the years we have held regular prayer evenings concentrating exclusively on the work of School of Ministries. A couple of years ago our ladies prayer group felt a surge of faith over the matter of finance and prayed seriously in faith for a breakthrough in provision. Since that time our finances seem to have always been in order and have been sufficient. We do not presume this will always be the case but testify to on-going provision from the most unlikely and unusual sources.

Thought to ponder: *What are you believing God to provide?*

14

DIFFICULT DAYS

Job 23:10. "But He knows the way that I take; when He has tried me, I shall come forth as gold."

Rom 5:3-5 We gladly suffer, because we know that suffering helps us to endure. And endurance builds character, which gives us a hope that will never disappoint us. All of this happens because God has given us the Holy Spirit, who fills our hearts with his love.

Heb. 12:10,11 "God corrects us for our own good, because he wants us to be holy, as he is. It is never fun to be corrected. In fact, at the time it is always painful. But if we learn to obey by being corrected, we will do right and live at peace."

Context

It is important that I add a chapter that contains some of the difficulties and other issues we have faced. It would be wrong of me to mislead you into thinking that we never had a problem or faced difficult situations.

The stories I have shared in this book have been over a period of some 70 years. I could write another one sharing the hardship and pressures we have encountered. That is not the purpose of this book. However, I am concerned that we live in a day where those who have been blessed and used by God suggest it is easy for us to experience the same success that they have enjoyed, without sharing the journey that resulted in the season of fruitfulness.

In our present day, the church led by Bill Johnson in Redding, California, known as Bethel, is receiving great press and rightly so. They are experiencing a move of the Holy Spirit. If we think we can copy what they do and enjoy success without paying the price that Bill has paid, we have not understood the ways of God.

I remember a brother, used by God in the Argentinian move of the Holy Spirit coming to the UK. He told the story of the revival how many had called on the Lord, fasted and prayed and been through difficult days before God had broken in with a wonderful move of the Holy Spirit. A song had been particularly used by God in the revival and he suggested that if we sang that song over and over it would result in us breaking through into revival.

I was immediately concerned because I do not believe God releases his power without the journey that precedes it. It is through the dealings of God in and through us, as expressed in the scriptures at the head of this chapter that God produces the character in us that allows the Holy Spirit to use us.

The apostle Paul lists a catalogue of suffering, opposition and persecution that accompanied his journey alongside the blessing, successes and miracles. *2Cor 11:23-30*. I do not intend to do that, but it is important to say that we have not journeyed without our share of challenges.

Pentecostal tradition

In the Pentecostal tradition in which I grew up, it was believed that strength was expressed in loud and challenging preaching, that anyone who had problems was weak, and the more aggressive you were the more anointed you were!

There was no room for vulnerability or weakness. In this atmosphere any sin or weakness was not confessed as judgement and exclusion followed. I had a problem with smoking as a teenager and on the few occasions I asked for help was just told to stop and looked down on. No prayer or counsel was offered, and it took a personal journey over several years to find freedom. There did not appear to be an understanding of the ways in which the Lord works in our lives.

Character flaws

However, through the experiences of life and the challenges of life, God has dealt with me over many issues in my life. The parenting of teenagers was a time of challenge for me. Situations I could not control, caused anxiety and fear, and brought to the surface weakness that resulted in me needing help and ministry.

The aggressive stance that had developed in me caused me to go through some difficulties. I began to ask God to release gentleness and patience as well as other "fruit of the Spirit" into my life. He is still not finished with me in those areas. The development of Godly character is a lifelong journey and requires our co-operation and it is often in the experiences of life that character is formed.

Finding God in some moments of fear and anxiety has been a part of the journey. On our second trip to China, we were visiting the city of Wuhan. We had visas for Shenzhen just over the border but had arranged to go on to Wuhan.

We were in China in January and had no idea just how cold it would be or that there was no heating in any of the houses or buildings. We flew into Wuhan from Shenzhen and as we landed were told to remain in our seats and have our passports ready for checking by the police.

Four large policemen entered the plane and began from the back of the plane checking each passenger's details. There was a scuffle, and one passenger was forcibly removed from the plane. As I sat there, I thought they had been warned about us and were looking for us. I began to feel a sense of fear as the police moved nearer to us. I spoke in tongues quietly waiting…. As I held out my passport to the authorities, they simply waved my hand aside without even looking at our papers.

My wife and Sylvia, our other lady companion did not experience any such fear. We then were taken to the church building where we were ministering. They provided us with a drink of hot water and some Chinese food from a stall that was awful and barely edible. We then needed to visit the bank. Sylvia, who was travelling with us needed to draw out money using her bankcard. She had been told back in the UK that her card could be used in China. We were freezing by this time and had no means of getting warm. I had previously travelled in July when it had been very hot. We were completely taken by surprise at this weather.

In 2002 I had undergone a triple by-pass operation on my heart. I was told there were two things that I must not do or allow to happen. One was to lift heavy weights the other was to allow my chest to get too cold. I began to imagine all kinds of things.

We then discovered that the credit card was incompatible with the Chinese banking system and could not be used. This caused us serious financial problems. We had also assumed we would have our accommodation covered only to find we had to pay our own costs. Now Sylvia had no way of paying her hotel costs and my cash was limited so once we had covered the hotel fees, we had only a few pounds left and at this stage did not know if our meals would be provided. There was also no way that we knew of acquiring any further money.

I went to bed that night with all this on my mind and it caused a dark cloud to descend on me. I thought I would die in this place, that no one would know we were here, that Irene would be left here with no means of getting home. It was the middle of the night. Eventually I woke Irene up and asked her to pray for me.

As she prayed, I felt a measure of relief. The next day we began the training programme with some 80 leaders. The Holy Spirit fell, and we had an extraordinary time of blessing as God worked in so many lives. During the first break in the morning, we were given three special, quilted coats that immediately solved the cold problem.

For 10 days we lived in these coats. Teaching, eating, sitting in a restaurant, always with our coats on. Food was provided for us, and we did not require any money as everything else was provided for us.

Praying always without ceasing

We have discovered that personal prayer is a key to coming through hardship and difficult situations. I am staggered at the number of believers who have not laid this foundation in their lives for when the storms come. One of the most dramatic answers to prayer when we were in trouble occurred when we were building an extension on one of our houses.

The builder had erected a scaffolding along the side of our house in our neighbour's garden without asking permission. Our neighbour was irritated by this, and it cause some friction between us. We agreed that the scaffolding would come down for the bank holiday weekend that was approaching.

As it approached the building work was not completed and when we requested our neighbour allowed us a couple more weeks, he lost his temper and threatened us with the law and even to dismantle the scaffolding himself and was demanding compensation. We began to pray… Seriously…

We encouraged the builder to complete the work by the required time and they agreed. It was all looking healthy, so we contacted the scaffolder to discover that he was not able to take it down due to an excessive amount of work. He was involved in an emergency job that demanded all his staff and plant over the weekend.

We were in a difficult position, and we cried out to God. We went to our neighbours and explained the position, the wife of the man of the house explained that this issue had caused problems in their marriage and that her husband was extremely angry. We prayed again, spending some time together calling on the Lord.

That evening at 6pm there was a caller at our door. I thought it was the man next door come to give me, at best a telling off, and at worst a beating. I suggested to Irene that she answered the door to which I received a short reply and went with some trepidation to answer the door. Imagine my surprise when I saw the owner of the scaffold company standing in our doorway.

He said, "I could not sleep last night, I was kept awake. I am not a believer in God, but a voice kept telling me that I should help this guy out and take down his scaffolding. So here I am. We will come at 6am in the morning and take it down." True to his word he had removed the works by 8am that morning and we were saved from a difficult situation.

I tell these stories to show that we have experienced hardship and difficulty and even some anxiety in our lives alongside the wonderful blessing of God. Our testimony is that God has helped us through many such times over these years. He has never failed us even in the most difficult situations.

Thought to ponder: *Recall an experience in your life where you overcame difficulty or a problem with God's help.*

15

SIGNIFICANT LEADERS

Heb 13:7. "Remember those leading you, who have spoken to you the Word of God, whose faith follow, considering the end of *their* conduct."

As the result of travelling around the world I have met with some amazing people and seen some exciting examples of Kingdom life and power. I recount some of those experiences. These are all first-hand encounters and have been an encouragement that has caused me to aspire to greater things for the God.

Menzie Oban

The first church I pastored was in Barnet, North London. During 1971 we had a visiting speaker called Menzie Oban. He was a Jamaican by birth who had come to England in the early 1950's. He had experienced a radical salvation from drug addiction whilst in London. He preached for us and shared his vision of returning to Jamaica to set up a ministry for drug addicts. I remember the message he preached. He made a great impression on me with his overwhelming passion and love for Jesus.

In 1985 I made my first visit to Jamaica. We were in the South of the island and the leader had arranged an itinerary for us. I noted we were to visit Montego Bay and asked our host if he knew Menzie Oban. The reply was that he was his best friend and that we would be staying with him when we visited that town.

We renewed our relationship with Menzie and each year I visited Jamaica I spent time with Menzie and his team. He developed a ministry known as Teamwork. There was a school, a church, a conference centre, agricultural projects, and a vision for the first trade school in the West Indies.

This man who had a basic education and had never been to any college, or had training in business, through faith and confidence in God's provision saw this massive project through, until there was property worth millions of pounds, built and paid for that fulfilled his vision. He was a joy to be with. He had an effervescent, joyful faith. He was outrageous and yet there was an attractiveness about his relationship with Jesus. He would burst into song at any moment.

I led a ministry trip to Jamaica consisting of around 12 young people. We arrived in the bustling airport in Montego Bay. In the crowd suddenly I heard the voice of Menzie above the hubbub. He shouted, "Brother Peter, Brother

Peter… Praise the Lord" He then proceeded to burst into singing the hymn "To God be the Glory". He sang the first verse and chorus! The team with me were overwhelmed! I do not think they had ever met his like as he gathered us into a rugby scrum to celebrate our arrival.

One year we were speaking at an Easter Convention. Following the meeting we went to an ice cream parlour. We purchased our ice creams and sat down to eat them. Menzie stood up in this crowded restaurant, clapped his hands and began to speak. He said, "You could not come to the meeting, so we are bringing the meeting to you. Easter is not about bun and cheese (an Easter custom similar to our Easter eggs) but about a man who died on the cross to bring you back into relationship with God." He then briefly encouraged people to receive the gospel and concluded with a prayer.

At the end of the prayer he said, "If this business is run on righteous lines, we ask you to bless it, if not please close it down". He then respectfully thanked everybody for listening and we enjoyed the rest of our ice cream. The next year when we visited Montego Bay the Ice Cream Parlour had ceased to trade!

On one visit to the UK, Irene and I felt we would like to buy him several pairs of shoes. He was insistent that we only buy him one pair of shoes and that the rest of the money should be given for their work amongst the poor in Jamaica. That is the measure of the man's heart for people.

Menzie lived until he was in his 80's and was used by God in the most extraordinary ways, it was a privilege to have met him.

John Beaumont

One day during a week at one of our camps, a couple of our Scottish friends advised us they had invited a friend from New Zealand who was staying close by to visit. They suggested that he was worth meeting. There were just a few of us who met with John Beaumont that afternoon. He was a quietly spoken and gentle man. As he came into the room there was an atmosphere of the presence of Jesus upon him; it was the first time that I sensed the presences of Jesus on someone in such a powerful way. There was an awesome sense of God on him as he shared.

We spoke about the Kingdom of God, and he shared some of the amazing stories of his experiences with Jesus. At the end of a couple of hours, he had to leave for an evening meeting and requested that he be allowed to lay hands on us. He went from person to person, laying his hands on our heads and quietly speaking in tongues.

I can only say that I felt the presence of God fill my life in a new and fresh way. An awareness of the nearness of Jesus touched me at that moment. John left the room and those of us who had been prayed for sat for a few minutes enjoying the fragrance of the presence of Jesus. It was an unforgettable moment. Over the next couple of years, we enjoyed John's company and ministry on several occasions.

John Noble

After a particularly difficult season I was asking the Lord how and where I should be connected for the next season of my life. I visited a Bible Week held at Pilgrims Hall,

Brentwood where the Team Spirit network of churches held an event. Several 1000 people were present, and John Noble was the leader of the event and hosted the meetings.

Many people took part, preached, led worship, prophesied, and brought their contribution. John opened the door for many others to ministry. John himself gave the notices and supported the band by playing the trumpet. As I watched him, I was filled with admiration for the humility and servant heart of this man. Most leaders I know would have taken the platform and preached at the main sessions; John was happy to take a back seat. I felt the Lord say I could trust this man with my life.

I joined his team several months later and served him in his work for some years. He later moved to another area, and we felt the Lord was calling us to stay where we were. However, I have never had reason to change my mind about this man of God and I still trust him and his judgement. Jesus said of Nathanael, *"Here is a real Israelite; there is nothing false in him!" John 1:47 GNB.* There are not many men I can say that about, but John is one of them.

Simeon Kayiwa

On my first trip to Uganda, I met Simeon Kayiwa. I sat for an afternoon with him listening to story after story of the miraculous, supernatural power of God being released through his ministry. He had seen dead people come to life, many infected with HIV declared free from infection, blind, deaf, and lame touched by God.

In 1985 when Uganda was in a state of unrest and in political and economic chaos, God spoke to Simeon in a powerful way and then used him to plant over 1000 churches in the nation. Miracles were the order of the day and I have met with people and heard their incredible stories. Some of them would not be out of place in the book of Acts. I have met many leaders from Uganda over the years and when I mention Simeon their reply is that "He is my father".

In those initial years it seems the Lord did extraordinary miracles. I only have room to record one of them. During the unrest many people began to spend the night in the church building as they were afraid their homes would be attacked by the secret police, or the army and they would lose their lives. There was no food in the markets or shops, and they had no money.

Simeon did not know what to do with the 150 people who had camped out in the building and had no food. Outside the building was a mango tree. It had never borne fruit even though it was a mature tree. Simeon says the Lord told him to command the tree to bear fruit. The next day it was laden with enough fruit for everybody and continued to bear fruit every day until food was available in the shops and markets.

I have seen the tree; it remains by the building and has never borne fruit since those days. Hearing stories of God's miraculous power being displayed in our day and generation is a tremendous encouragement. Still today there is a queue of people who come every day to be prayed with at Narimembe Christian Fellowship.

Miracles are still happening, and people are still being set free.

The ladies of Lujizweni

We had another experience of encountering the presence of God when we visited South Africa. We visited a village some 30 kilometres from the city of Umtata. There was no electricity or running water and most of the people lived in "rondavels" (round mud huts with straw or tin roofs.)

I had taken a team from the UK to teach and train in both spiritual and social activities. During the week we were invited to a special rondavel where we were told a story of a move of the Holy Spirit that had commenced some years before.

A group of ladies had felt called to prayer until revival came. They had built this rondavel with their own hands and dedicated it to prayer. They arranged their affairs so they could gather and pray until God came. They were simple folks and did not know that after 40 days without food your body shuts down and so continued in their quest. It was after 80 days that the presence of God broke in among them.

They told us the roof of the hut was raised some 3 feet in the air and lightning crashed against the walls bouncing from side to side. They were all on their faces for a further 10 days. The presence of God was so powerful that people walking past the hut up to 100 yards away were touched by the presence of God and fell on their faces calling on God to save them.

They testified that people who were demon possessed ran towards the building and were instantly delivered as they encountered the power of God. Resulting from that experience the whole region was impacted over the next years with many churches being planted to contain and disciple the new converts, the dead were raised, and many healings took place. Lujizweni became an oasis to many who travelled to encounter the presence of God. We visited as this move of the Spirit was receding but still there was a sense of God around the area.

When we were told this story in the actual hut where it had happened, we were touched by God. The rondavel had a mud floor but those of us who heard the story laid on the floor on our faces as the Lord touched our hearts afresh with a desire to know such a move of the Holy Spirit.

These ladies made such an impression on me. They had nothing in the way of material things, most of them were older women who had suffered hardship, been abused, left by their husbands with children to cope on their own and yet they were some of the most contented and happy people I have ever met.

Thomas Mahlelempini and Cliff Mthembu

Other significant leaders I met in South Africa were Thomas and Cliff. Thomas was the old fashioned, simple evangelist totally dependent on the Holy Spirit. He had a dream. Sometime later he passed through the township of Kwa Debeka near Pinetown and saw the place that was in his dream so moved to the area and planted a church. He held a crusade, gathered people together and saw a church grow.

He did something similar around the area that is now known as the Eastern Cape. Stories of miracles, provision and healing surrounded this man who was tragically taken from us at 61 in a head on car accident.

Cliff took on the work. He is an educated man who held a very high position in social services before taking on the leadership of the churches. They have more than doubled since he took on the apostolic leadership of the movement.

He moves in miracles and has seen God work prolifically through these last years. I have watched and admired this man, who is my friend. He has become a stateman leader carrying a great anointing.

Myles Munroe

I had the privilege over some years of connecting with Myles Munroe from the Bahamas. His impact on my life from the moment we met was very significant. He inspired me to believe that I could achieve far more than I was at that time and lifted my expectation of what God could do through me. His inspirational, prophetic preaching alongside his personal encouragement were a spur to greater things for God.

Joel Laurore

I met this man from Haiti in Montego Bay, Jamaica. We were invited to preach together at a teaching conference for the church in Western Jamaica. He stood to speak. He held a pad of yellow paper in front of him and began to read several scriptures and make a few comments. It was very ordinary and very disjointed, and I found myself thinking. "Who is the guy?"

Suddenly, everything changed. I have never seen the anointing of the Holy Spirit fall so visibly and dramatically on anyone. He stopped and cried out as the Spirit visibly touched him and then proceeded for 90 minutes to preach, prophecy, sing, pray and generally connect with God and with those of us who were listening. At the end of his preach he was totally exhausted and covered in perspiration. He had lost so much fluid that it was poured out from his shoes. It was an extraordinary experience.

That evening, as we were in the same accommodation, Irene and I spent some time with this unusual man. We started talking at around 10pm in the evening and did not go to bed until 5am the next morning. We have never done that with anyone before or since. He told us his story.

He had been a baptist minister in Haiti. He had gone to the USA and trained in their Theological colleges and was highly educated with various degrees in Theology. The Baptist Union had requested he take on the leadership of their Western African Theological college located in Liberia.

He agreed to this appointment and spent 10 years leading the college. There were some 150 students from as many as 35 nations in the college. Each Monday evening, he would address the student body.

One evening he sat in his study and talked with the Lord. The conversation went something like, "Lord, after 10 years I have nothing left to give. If you do not turn up this evening and empower me by your Holy Spirit, I am going home to become a schoolteacher."

He went out to the student body and as he began to speak the Holy Spirit came upon him and he began to speak in tongues. For the next three hours he spoke in tongues and later found out that he had prophesied over every student in their own language. That meant 150 prophecies in 35 different African languages.

He told us that the students told him he was lifted off the ground as he spoke. This was the beginning of a move of the Holy Spirit in Liberia which resulted in many coming to Jesus and supernatural outpouring of healings and miracles. This continued for several years.

We shared with him our own story, we prayed for our families, we wept together and experienced another one of those moments when the presence of God is intense. We have met with Joel on several occasions since and thank God for the privilege of meeting him. He touched our lives.

Many others have impacted our lives and time would fail to tell of their input and encouragement, but we thank everyone who has helped, influenced, and supported us on the journey.

Thought to ponder: *Who has helped you, influenced you for good, discipled you or impacted your life?*

16

ADVICE FROM AN OLD FOGEY

2 Tim 2:2. "You have often heard me teach. Now I want you to tell these same things to followers who can be trusted to tell others."

In recent days I have received three distinct prophetic words about this next season. Christy Wimber (daughter of John Wimber) called me out at a Pioneer conference some 3 years ago and suggested that I was not finished yet but had a contribution to make in encouraging the next generation of leaders.

At our recent meeting to celebrate the work of SOM and for me to step down from leading the ministry Graham Blake brought the same word.

A couple of weeks later another friend, Paul Turner shared the same thought in an email that he had felt inspired to send. I trust that our journey will be that. Here are a few more thoughts along that line.

Read your Bible... pray every day

As children, the words of the above song were "drummed" into us, maybe it was in a legalistic way and did not produce fruit but there is a grace from God and a desire for God that will result in spending time in the Bible and the presence of God every day.

Both Joshua and the first Psalm emphasise the importance of day and night meditation on the things of God. This is essential if you are to be successful and fruitful in any ministry. That is what the scriptures says:

Josh 1:8. "This Book of the Law shall not depart from your mouth, but you shall meditate on it day and night, so that you may be careful to do according to all that is written in it. For then you will make your way prosperous, and then you will have good success."

Follow the will of God regardless of the cost

Matt 6:33. "But seek first the kingdom of God and His righteousness; and all these things shall be added to you."

Never make decisions based on financial issues, particularly the lack of money. Faith demands that we trust God and if he has clearly revealed His will, He can be trusted to provide everything you need to do what He says. His promise is that He will not let you down. That is our experience

Include your wife/husband in your life and decision making

Do everything you can to create harmony in your home. There are enough pressures from church leadership and the enemy who seeks to bring you down, without experiencing chaos and antagonism in your home. It needs to be a haven, an oasis, a place where you can rest.

Include your wife or husband in every major decision, if they are not with you, it will be a major hindrance. There are times and some decisions where your children should also be part of the decision-making process. The fulfilment of your vision and assignment depends on you taking your family with you!

Don't neglect your family

I say this with hindsight. One of the things I would change about my life is the time I spent prioritising meetings over my wife and family.

I would spend more time with them, making more room for them. Protecting them from some of the pressures of being "leader's kids".

I remember one of my friends whose daughter had been made pregnant by a guy in the church who happened to be married. I asked him how he handled that, having the guy in the church. His reply shocked me and yet maybe it is the right response.

He said, "I told him if he showed his face in this church again, I would punch his lights out". That might be extreme, but I do believe we should protect our children.

Watch your time.

It is important to live a disciplined life. Many leaders are not on an 8-hour day, 40-hour week but nevertheless need to be disciplined.

I believe I have achieved more than many others because of maintaining a regular framework and order. Scripture reading and prayer first thing in the morning.

Study on regular days, meetings on regular days where it is possible. It was an interesting time when I had my heart by-pass operation. I felt the Lord give me a simple but important word it was "Do less but achieve more".

I believe that opened the door for me to concentrate on the major focus of my calling which was teaching and training of leaders and not get taken up with the multiplicity of other stuff that comes with running church.

Discover your calling.

What is your calling? I took years to discover mine even though I knew I was called to ministry and leadership. It is summed up in three words; Teach, train, travel.

Following my heart operation, I stopped driving to meetings all over the country just to preach. It might have been good for my ego, but it was debilitating and exhausting. I would arrive back at some very late hour and then work a full day. I do not believe it was what the Lord intended for me.

I wrote to all the churches I visited following my heart operation and said I would only visit if I was involved with teaching and training as well as preaching. This was misunderstood by some, but I believe was essential. Many leaders experience "burn out" or even worse because they are doing stuff that God has never called them to.

Disciple the people.

I have written a booklet in which I outline my understanding of effective leadership principles. They are: Discover your purpose; Define your vision; Develop the team; Disciple the people and Transform the community.

I am not suggesting that these 5 issues are the only building blocks. I believe there are other priorities that also need to be in place. Basic spiritual disciplines of prayer, outreach, teaching, training, organisation, and structure are foundational, but I believe for leaders these 5 matters are essential.

These are not the only five, but these five elements are necessary for successful and effective leadership, to build the kind of churches that are going to grow and last. Our primary calling is to "make disciples".

That's it… The meanderings and memories of the journey we have been on. We are nearer our destination than we ever have been but continue to "keep right on to the end of the road."

Phil. 3:14 *"I press toward the mark for the prize of the high calling of God in Christ Jesus."*

I trust there has been something in this book that has encouraged your faith in a God who loves you, cares for you and will fulfil His purpose through you.

I love You, Lord
For Your mercy never fails me
All my days, I've been held in Your hands
From the moment that I wake up
Until I lay my head
Oh, I will sing of the goodness of God

And all my life You have been faithful
And all my life You have been so, so good
With every breath that I am able
Oh, I will sing of the goodness of God

I love Your voice
You have led me through the fire
In the darkest night
You are close like no other
I've known You as a Father
I've known You as a Friend
And I have lived in the goodness of God

And all my life You have been faithful
And all my life You have been so, so good
With every breath that I am able

OUR JOURNEY

Oh, I will sing of the goodness of God

Your goodness is running after
It's running after me
Your goodness is running after
It's running after me
With my life laid down
I'm surrendered now
I give You everything
Your goodness is running after
It's running after me

And all my life You have been faithful
And all my life You have been so, so good
With every breath that I am able
I will sing of the goodness of God.

Copyright 2019 Bethel Music

ABOUT THE AUTHOR

Peter Butt trained in the Assemblies of God Bible College. Since 1970 he has been involved in church leadership. He founded and established the School of Ministries leadership training programme out of New Community Church, Southampton. He travels widely nationally and internationally training leaders as well as overseeing churches in the UK. He is married to Irene and has four married children, seven grandchildren and four great grandchildren.

Also, if you haven't already read them, take a look at Peter's other books:

For all UK orders please use the following links, otherwise please go to Amazon.com.

"Pentecost Now… Pentecost Then…" – *A Fresh Look at the Person and Work of the Holy Spirit Today:* https://geni.us/pnpt

"Pentecost Expressed" – *A Fresh Look at the Gifts of the Holy Spirit:* https://geni.us/pentecostexpressed

"Pentecost Released" – *A Fresh Look at Leadership in Acts and The Early Church:* https://geni.us/pentecostreleased

www.jascottpublications.com/peterbutt